D1277525

iNTER_ACTiVE

English as a Second Language   **Secondary Cycle One**

Student Book

B

Carole Gauthier
Gwenn Gauthier
Michael O'Neill
Leena M. Sandblom, Series Co-ordinator

LES ÉDITIONS
CEC
QUEBECOR MEDIA

8101, boul. Métropolitain Est, Anjou (Québec) Canada H1J 1J9
Téléphone : (514) 351-6010 • Télécopieur : (514) 351-3534

Editorial Manager, ESL
Julie Hough

Production Manager
Danielle Latendresse

Project Editors
Michèle Devlin
Angel Beyde

Proofreader
Joseph Shragge

Rights research
Shona French

Cover and page layout
Dessine-moi un mouton

Page design
Diabolo-Menthe

Illustrations
Martin Goneau, Vincent Régimbald, Michel Lebrun

Maps
Claude Bernard

DANGER

LE PHOTOCOPILLAGE TUE LE LIVRE

La *Loi sur le droit d'auteur* interdit la reproduction d'œuvres sans l'autorisation des titulaires des droits. Or, la photocopie non autorisée – le photocopillage – a pris une ampleur telle que l'édition d'œuvres nouvelles est mise en péril. Nous rappelons donc que toute reproduction, partielle ou totale, du présent ouvrage est interdite sans l'autorisation écrite de l'Éditeur.

Les Éditions CEC inc. remercient le gouvernement du Québec de l'aide financière accordée à l'édition de cet ouvrage par l'entremise du Programme de crédit d'impôt pour l'édition de livres, administré par la SODEC.

Inter_Active, Student Book B
© 2006, Les Éditions CEC inc.
8101, boul. Métropolitain Est
Anjou (Québec) H1J 1J9

Tous droits réservés. Il est interdit de reproduire, d'adapter ou de traduire l'ensemble ou toute partie de cet ouvrage sans l'autorisation écrite du propriétaire du copyright.

Dépôt légal : 2006
Bibliothèque et Archives nationales du Québec
Bibliothèque et Archives du Canada

ISBN: 2-7617-1791-0

Imprimé au Canada
1   2   3   4   5   10   09   08   07   06

Acknowledgements

The authors wish to thank Les Éditions CEC for their unfailing support. Heartfelt thanks go to Julie Hough who, with good humour and steadfast determination, led us through the dense forest of this project, and to the editorial staff for their excellent input and timely suggestions. Many thanks to everyone at Dessine-moi un mouton for producing a beautiful book and to Danielle Latendresse for making the process smooth.

Special thanks go to the students and staff members at Heritage Regional High School who took part in our video recordings.

Personal thanks to the following people:
To my husband Marc, to Karine and François and my father Roméo Gauthier, for their love and encouragement throughout all my writing projects. And to everyone who participated in the realization of this project for their insightful ideas, comments and suggestions. – CG

To all the pedagogues in my life,
To all my family and friends, endless source of inspiration,
And to GPB for your faith in me — sincere thanks. – GG

To my co-authors and editors with whom several excellent ESL materials were produced over the past fifteen years. To the fine staff and management at Les Éditions CEC who gave me the opportunity to write books. And to Ana for her love and understanding. – MON

I wish to acknowledge three great second-language pedagogues. They were my mentors whether they knew it or not: Pierre Calvé, Monique Duplantie, Roger Tremblay. I learned so much from you. Then, I found my own voice. Thank you.
I acknowledge my coauthors for their doggedness and good cheer throughout the *Inter_Active* years. It was a joy to work with you, to share grand laughs together, and sometimes a tear. I acknowledge and thank Julie Hough for simply everything.
I thank my friend Carole Lafrance, for being there and cheering me on. And finally, the one whose spirit surrounded me on the good days and the bad, Stanley G. French. – LMS

Special thanks to all who made the Unit 1 Expedition photographs possible: The Boily-Lachance family (Marc-Étienne, Jasmin, Chloé, Mathieu, Jean-Réné, Annie), Sabrina Mathieu, Laurent Moreau, Claude Mathieu (Pub Photo Inc.).

TABLE OF CONTENTS

YOUR STUDENT BOOK

Here is what you will find in this book.

There are 12 units with great themes you can relate to, including two fun projects.

● **The first page of each unit** introduces the theme of the unit.

• Fast Forward activities help you discover what you will do and learn in the unit.

FAST FORWARD ▶▶▶

● **The other activity pages** let you explore the theme of the unit and learn new language.

• Glossaries list unfamiliar words and their meaning.

• Strategy boxes introduce helpful strategies for reading, writing and speaking English.

• Culture Pop-Up boxes offer interesting information about English usage and culture.

• Helpful Language boxes suggest appropriate vocabulary and expressions.

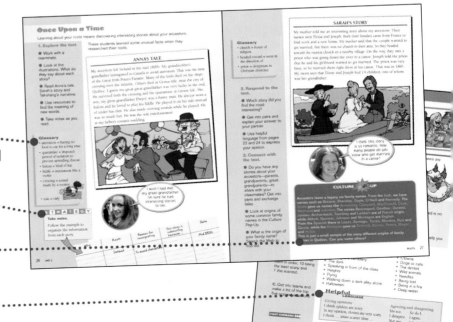

Now You're Talking pages

focus on conversations.

- Language models introduce new expressions.
- Recordings let you listen to authentic conversations.
- A practice activity lets you use similar language in conversations with your classmates.

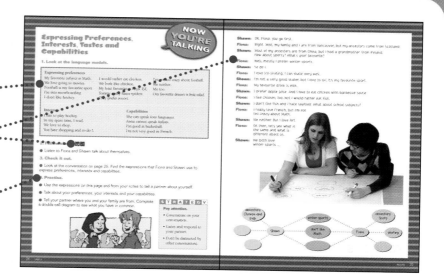

Focus on Form pages

review or introduce you to the grammar you need to communicate about the theme.

- An introductory activity shows you how much you already know.
- Charts explain basic grammar rules and offer specific examples.
- A practice activity lets you use the grammar in context.
- Heads Up boxes remind you of useful strategies, suggest resources or provide additional information.

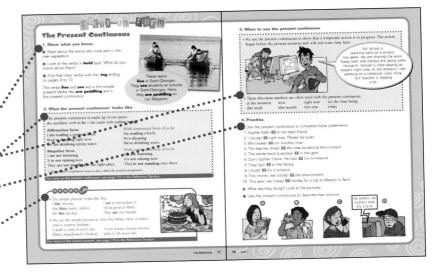

End-of-unit tasks

give you an opportunity to use the language and information from the unit to do more complex activities.

- This box reminds you to add new words from the unit to your vocabulary log.
- Rewind activities help you evaluate what you learned.

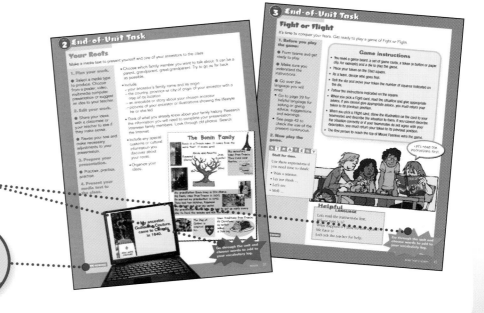

● **Project units** let you work creatively with classmates on assignments that reflect your interests and abilities. ....

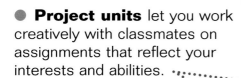
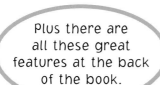
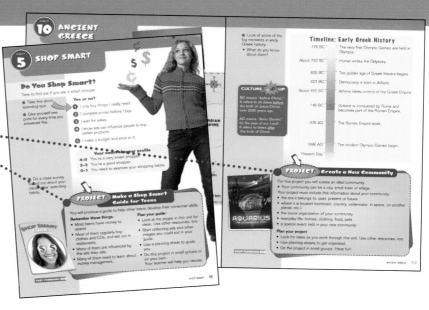

Plus there are all these great features at the back of the book.

● **An anthology section** has poems and stories that will help you improve your reading skills. ....

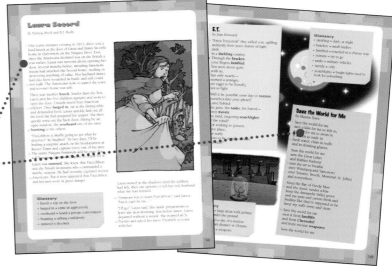

● **A reference section** provides some useful tools:

- Illustrated vocabulary charts explain the thematic vocabulary for each unit. ....

- Grammar charts review the various grammatical rules you need to know. ....

- Strategy and process charts show you how to communicate efficiently in English. ....

- Functional language charts group together useful expressions. ....

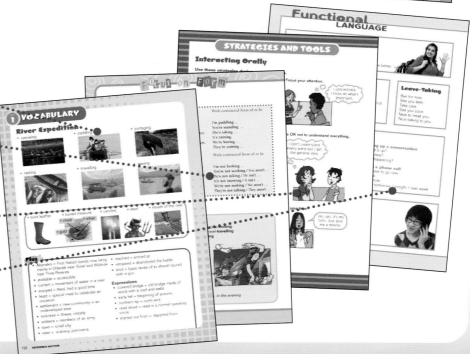

THE EXPEDITION

What Did You Do Last Summer?

How was your summer? Great? Good? So-so?

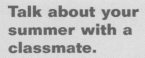

Talk about your summer with a classmate.

● What activity was the most fun? What was the best adventure?

● What was the most boring activity? The worst day of the summer?

● What places did you visit? What was the best place?

● What movies did you see? What was the best movie?

● What new people did you meet? Who was the most interesting person?

swimming and diving

camping

meeting new friends

delivering papers

singing and making music

bicycling

visiting

mowing the lawn

Glossary
• so-so = not good, but not bad

Helpful LANGUAGE

I had lots of fun ...	I really hated ...	He was very ...
I went to ...	I visited ...	They were ...
I saw ...	I met ...	

River Expedition: Present and Past

Canoeing can be a fun activity as well as a learning experience. A group of teenagers went canoeing with a mission. They followed the path of a historic expedition.

1. Explore the text.

HEADS uP

Always start by exploring a text before you read it all.

In 1775, Benedict Arnold, an American colonel, led 1100 soldiers to attack the city of Québec. In the early fall of 2005, five teens from the Beauce region visited scenes of that military expedition.

● Look at the title and illustrations. What do they tell you?

● There are two sections to this story.
  • When do the events in the photos take place?
  • When do the events in the illustrations take place?

● Read paragraphs 1 and 2 on page 9. What do they tell you?

● Look for words you know. What do they tell you?

● Predict what the text is about.

● Read each sentence. Stop and ask yourself if you understand it.

● Use resources for words you don't know: the glossaries, the vocabulary list on page 160 and your dictionary.

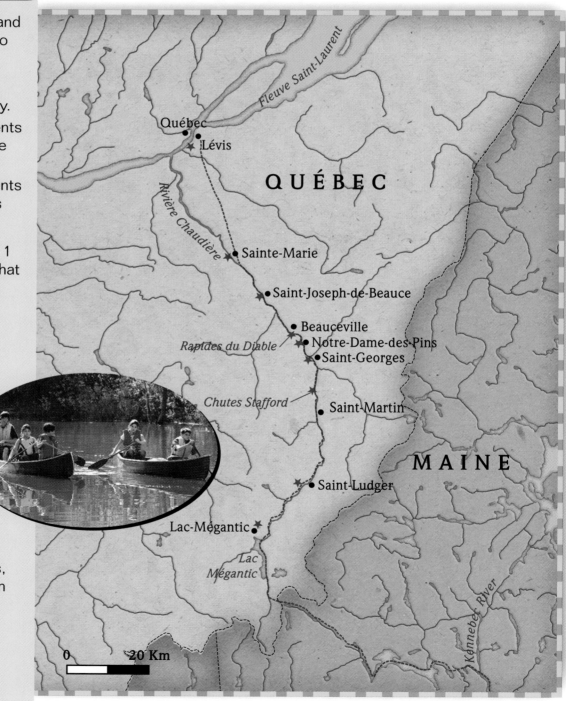

1 These teens live in Saint-Georges. Their names are Mathieu, Chloé, Jasmin, Marc-Étienne and Sabrina. Their objective is to follow the path of Arnold's expedition on the Kennebec River and Rivière Chaudière.

2 This is Benedict Arnold. He was a general in the army of the 13 American colonies. On September 11, 1775, he started out from Massachusetts with 1100 soldiers. His mission was to conquer Québec and make it the 14th American colony.

3 Here, the teens are paddling on Lac Mégantic. They are doing fine because there is no wind. When it is windy, this large lake can be dangerous for canoes. What a view!

4 Arnold travelled north on the Kennebec River toward Lac Mégantic in October 1775.

5 This is a view of Lac-Mégantic, a town near the site of Arnold's camp.

6 Arnold spent a few days at the northern tip of the lake resting his troops. Food supplies were low and his troops were hungry. They had to eat dogs, candles and boot leather to survive.

Glossary
- path = footsteps, itinerary
- toward = in the direction of

7 The teens are cruising up Rivière Chaudière on a beautiful day.

8 Arnold and his men travelled up Rivière Chaudière. This was an easy part of the river for them, too. But watch out!

9 Here they are having a good look at this dangerous part of the river. They are planning their route. They are not repeating Arnold's mistake. No canoes here!

10 What a disaster! Arnold lost four boats in the Chutes Stafford rapids.

11 The group is exploring an island near the spot where Arnold's camp was located. It is near the centre of Saint-Georges, a busy city.

12 With the help of the strong current, Arnold's expedition reached Sartigan, an Indian settlement. They camped at the mouth of Rivière Famine. The Abenakis gave them much-needed food.

Glossary
- cruising = travelling without difficulty
- watch out = be careful
- spot = place

13 Chloé and Sabrina are paddling under the old bridge at Notre-Dame-des-Pins. This is the longest covered bridge in Québec.

14 Arnold and his men travelled quickly up this part of the river.

15 Chloé and Mathieu are portaging around the dangerous Rapides du Diable. Legend says there is buried treasure here.

16 They lost a chest filled with gold and silver in the rapids. Many people have tried to find the treasure. But legend has it that the devil protects the treasure. That's where the name of these rapids comes from.

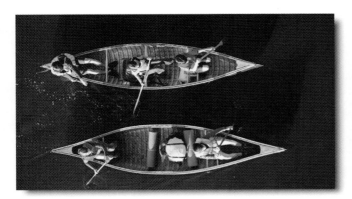

17 The group is travelling up the river. They are going under the bridge at Saint-Joseph-de-Beauce.

18 The river became calmer at last. And food was now easily available for Arnold's soldiers.

Glossary
• chest = large, strong box

19 The teens are visiting Sainte-Marie. They are standing in front of the church and celebrating the success of their expedition.

21 The teens are admiring the beautiful view of Old Québec.

23 All five teens enjoyed their river expedition. They thought the Arnold expedition was fascinating.

20 On November 6, the expedition camped at a spot near Sainte-Marie. The local residents organized a feast for Arnold and his officers.

22 The expedition pushed on to Pointe-Lévy. They arrived in mid-November. Here, they rested and prepared for battle. Many soldiers died of sickness.

24 Arnold and his small army of 700 attacked Québec during a snowstorm on December 30. Arnold was shot in the leg. Another American general named Montgomery was killed. Arnold and his men retreated. Québec did not become an American state.

2. Respond to the text.

● Answer the questions without looking at the text.

● Compare answers with a classmate.

● Now scan through the text to check your answers.

3. Connect with the text.

● Have you ever canoed or participated in an outdoors adventure like hiking, cycling or kayaking?

● Share your experience with your group.

4. Go beyond the text.

● Canada has lots of rivers, but many of them have serious problems. Look at illustrations A and B. What's wrong with each picture?

● What are the names of the rivers in your region?

● Are the rivers clean? Can you swim in them?

● Who pollutes these rivers? People, cities, farms, industry?

1. What are the names of the teens who took part in the canoeing expedition?
2. When did the Arnold expedition leave Massachusetts?
3. What is the name of the large lake that the teens paddled across?
4. What two rivers did Arnold travel on to get to the city of Québec?
5. What is a portage?
6. How many boats did the expedition lose near Chutes Stafford?
7. What do people look for near the Rapides du Diable?
8. Where is the longest covered bridge in Québec?
9. Where did Arnold and his troops stop to prepare for battle?
10. Did Benedict Arnold win the Battle of Québec?

Helpful LANGUAGE

I had the same experience as …
I went …
It was …

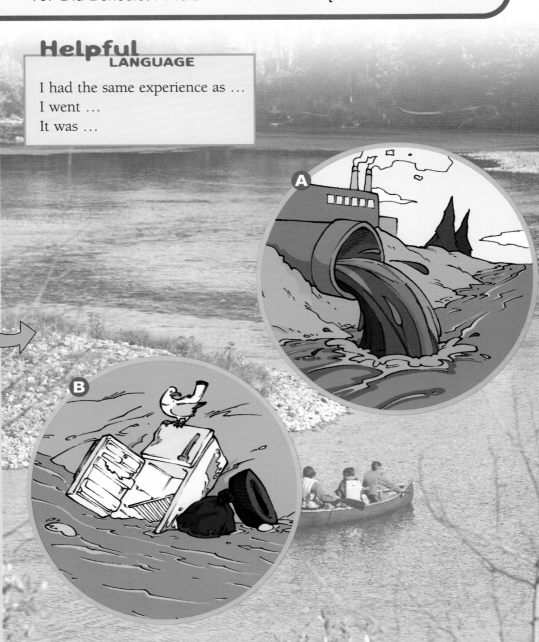

5. Extension

● Find your region on the map below.

● Do you recognize the names from your region? What other places have English names in your region?

● Find out why they have these names. Visit your school library or local library.

● Report back to the class.

CULTURE P🌟P-UP

Here, Chloé admires the power and the beauty of the Chutes Stafford. Stafford is an English name. The falls are named after a town in the middle of England.

In each region there are places and streets with English names.

These English names are there for historical and geographical reasons. They are named after people who lived there or were important for other reasons. The name may also be the same as the name of an English place elsewhere in the world.

Saguenay – Lac-Saint-Jean
Riverbend, Lac Connelly

Mauricie
Saint-Thomas-de-Caxton, Hunterstown, Red Mill

Centre-du-Québec
Saint-Cyrille-de-Wendover, Saint-Léonard-d'Aston, Kingsey Falls

Abitibi-Témiscamingue
Sullivan, McWatters

Outaouais
Wakefield, Buckingham

Laval – Lanaudière – Laurentides
New Glasgow, Rawdon

Montréal
Beaconsfield, Westmount

City of Québec and area
Shannon, Stoneham, Tewkesbury

Charlevoix
Saint-Fidèle-de-Mont-Murray

Duplessis
Magpie, Clarke City, Forestville

Bas-Saint-Laurent – Gaspesie – Îles-de-la-Madeleine
Douglastown, New-Carlisle

Chaudière-Appalaches
Saint-Prosper-de-Dorchester, Armagh

Estrie
Bury, Stornoway

Montérégie
Otterburn Park, Saint-Paul-d'Abbotsford, Hudson

Let's Talk

It is the beginning of the school year. This is one of your first English classes. Get to know your classmates, in English.

1. Look at the language models.

Greetings, introductions and leave-taking

Hi, there.   Bye for now.   Where are you from?
Fine.   See you later.   Nice to meet you.
My name is ...   Hi, how are you?   Pleased to meet you.
Are you a new student?   OK, I guess.   Nice talking to you.
This is ...   What is your name?   See you soon.

2. Follow along.

Mia: Hi, there. My name is Mia. What's your name?

Jeff: Oh, hi. It's Jeffrey, but my friends call me Jeff.

Mia: Are you a new student?

Jeff: Yes. We moved here in July from Montréal.

Mia: Well, this is my friend Alex. Alex, this is Jeff.

Alex: Hi, Jeff. That's a nice design on your shirt.

Jeff: That's the logo of my hockey team. Do you play hockey?

Alex: No, but I love volleyball. I hope that there's a team.

Mia: There is. I hope you make the team.

Alex: Well, I've got to go. Nice talking to you.

Jeff: Me too. Nice meeting you. Bye.

Mia: Bye, Jeff. See you later, Alex.

3. Check it out.

● Look at the conversation.

• How did Mia and Jeff greet each other? What expressions did they use?

• How did Mia introduce Jeff to Alex?

• How did they say good-bye? What expressions did they use?

4. Practise.

- Introduce yourself to your partner.

- Introduce your partner to another pair of students.

- Talk about yourself a bit. Find out about your classmates' interests.

- Use greetings and expressions for leave-taking.

- Use resources: the language models and conversation on page 15 and the strategies on this page.

STRATEGY

Don't forget to use strategies to help you communicate in English.

- Look at the situations below. Which of these strategies are the students using?

1. Plan and practise.
2. Use gestures.
3. Ask for help.
4. Use what you know.
5. Take your time.
6. Use resources.
7. Take chances.
8. Say it differently.
9. Be cool.
10. Encourage yourself.

A He was very tall.

B I know I can do this.

C First I say ... Then, ... I need these words and this question.

D I already know these words... space rocket mission astronaut

E I think I know this.

F I don't know this. But I know where to find what I need.

G I don't know what to say. I will ask someone to help me.

H Yes, yes. It's my turn. Just give me a minute.

I Hmm. What's that word? He's the leader of the football team. You know the ...

J Don't panic. Remain calm.

Focus on Form

The Present Continuous

1. Show what you know.

● Read about the teens who took part in the river expedition.

● Look at the verbs in **bold** type. What do you notice about them?

● Find five other verbs with the **-ing** ending on pages 9 to 12.

The verbs **live** and **are** are in the simple present. Verbs like **are paddling** are in the present continuous.

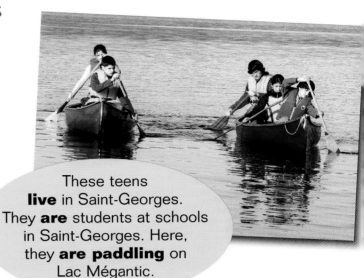

These teens **live** in Saint-Georges. They **are** students at schools in Saint-Georges. Here, they **are paddling** on Lac Mégantic.

2. What the present continuous* looks like

The present continuous is made up of two parts:
the auxiliary verb **to be** + the main verb ending in **ing**

Affirmative form
I **am reading** a mystery book.
Brad **is sleeping** right now.
We **are drinking** spring water.

With contracted form of *to be*
I**'m reading** a book.
He**'s sleeping**.
We**'re drinking** water.

Negative form
I **am not listening**.
It **is not raining** now.
They **are not standing** in the right place.

With contracted form of *to be*
I**'m not listening**.
It**'s not raining** now.
They**'re not standing** over there.

* The present continuous tense is also called the present progressive.

For more on the present continuous, see page 172 in the Reference Section.

HEADS UP

• The simple present looks like this:
I **like** movies.
She **likes** music videos.
We **like** hockey.

I **am** in Secondary II.
He **is** great at Math.
They **are** my friends.

• We use the simple present to describe habits, facts or states and to express feelings.
I walk to school every day.
Mike's skateboard is broken.

I love science fiction movies.
Julie is 14 years old.

For more on the simple present, see page 170 in the Reference Section.

3. When to use the present continuous

- We use the present continuous to show that a temporary action is in progress. The action began before the present moment and will end some time later.

> Our group is working hard on a project this week. We are sharing the work. Today Matt and Daniela are doing some research. William is interviewing an expert right now. At the moment, I am working on a computer slide show. Our teacher is helping a lot.

- These discourse markers are often used with the present continuous.

at the moment	now	right now	for the time being
this week	this month	this year	today

4. Practise.

A. Use the present continuous to complete these statements.

1. Sophie (talk) **?** to her best friend.
2. I (study) **?** right now. Please be quiet.
3. We (make) **?** our lunches now.
4. The teacher (help) **?** the new student at the moment.
5. The whole band (practise) **?** in the gym.
6. Don't bother Steve. He (do) **?** his homework.
7. They (go) **?** to the library.
8. I (look) **?** for a solution.
9. This month, we (study) **?** the environment.
10. This year, we (raise) **?** money for a trip to Mexico in April.

B. What are they doing? Look at the pictures.

● Use the present continuous to describe their actions.

A

B

C

D

> He shoots, he scores! And it's 3 to 0!

End-of-Unit Task

What's Going On?

Picture yourself in this school cafeteria. Write about what is happening.

1. Prepare to write.

● Look at the illustration carefully.

● Answer these questions and take notes.
- What are you doing?
- Who are the other people in the scene? Give them names.
- What are they doing? Make up some interesting details.

2. Write a first draft.

● Look at the example.

● Use the present continuous to describe what is happening.

3. Revise your text.

● Read your text and look for errors.

● Write your final copy.

4. Go public.

● Share with your group by reading your text aloud.

> I am walking into the cafeteria. My friend Jana is waving at me. She is wearing a great top. Ben is eating a huge banana sandwich. Jessie and Brent are talking on their cellphones again. Sophie is listening to rap music <u>and</u> doing her English homework. The twins, Bart and Brad, are ...

HEADS UP

Using a writing process will improve the quality of your writing.

1. Prepare to write: take notes and organize your ideas.
2. Write a first draft.
3. Revise your text and then write your final copy.
4. Go public. Share your text with your classmates.

◀◀◀ REWIND

Go through the unit and choose words to add to your vocabulary log.

Where Do You Come From?

How well do you know your family's roots? Where do your ancestors come from?

QUÉBEC

Rouyn-Noranda

Fleuve Saint-Laurent

Gaspé •

QUÉBEC

• Québec

Montréal • • Odanak
Lennoxville • CANTONS-DE-L'EST

0   150 km

• Ottawa

1 My name is John. My family is Abenaki. We are from Odanak.

DENMAR
NETHERLANDS

UNITED KINGDOM
Dublin •
• Amsterdam
London •
IRELAND
Paris •
FRANCE

2 I'm Marjorie. My family comes from Lennoxville.

• Washington

USA

ATLANTIC OCEAN

HAITI
Cap-Haïtien •
Port-au-Prince •

SOUTH AMERICA

3 My name is Nadine and we come from Haiti.

Libreville •
GABON

PERU

A. Look at the map of the world.

● Read about the origins of each teen.

● Tell a classmate about your origins.

B. We are a multicultural nation. Where do we come from?

● Match the nationality to the country.

● Find these countries on the map and say which continent they are in.

A. Greek	1. Hungary
B. American	2. China
C. Danish	3. The United Kingdom
D. Thai	4. Peru
E. Chinese	5. The Netherlands
F. Gabonese	6. Thailand
G. Dutch	7. Greece
H. Peruvian	8. Denmark
I. Hungarian	9. Gabon
J. British	10. The United States

FAST FORWARD ▶▶▶

I Am Canadian

Meet four teens with different roots but very similar lives.

1. Explore the text.

● On your own, skim through the texts. List the name of each teen and where their ancestors came from.

● With a partner, compare your answers.

● If you disagree, go back and check the texts.

2. Respond to the text.

● Choose two teens and read the texts again.

● Compare the teens. What is the same and what is different about them?

My name is Marc-Anthony, but my friends call me Marky. I'm 16 years old and I'm in Secondary V. My ancestors are Italian. I speak English, French, Italian and a bit of Spanish. My favourite subjects are Gym and Science and Technology. I like to play football but I prefer soccer, and in my spare time I deejay for school dances. I really like music a lot. I also like to fix things. I love pizza, lasagna and cheeseburgers. I've been to Italy once already and hope to go again after high school.

I'm Virginie and I'm in Secondary III. I am 14 years old. I was born in Canada, but my mom comes from Belgium and my dad is from Germany. My father can speak six languages. I speak two: English and French. I've already been to Europe to learn about my roots. I plan to go again when I finish school. My favourite things include Geography, soccer, dancing, lasagna and shepherd's pie with a tall glass of iced tea. Math is my least favourite subject, and I hate it when people talk too much. In my spare time I like to watch movies and hang out with my friends.

STRATEGY

Compare.

Make a double-cell diagram in your notebook and use it to make your comparisons. Follow the model.

Double-Cell Diagram

Same

Different   **Different**

ancestors German and Belgian

Soccer   ancestors Italian

Virginie   English and French   Marc-Anthony

Glossary

- deejay = play music at a dance or on the radio
- pet peeve = a minor irritation
- bite their nails =

My name is Anna and I'm 13 years old. I love my Dance and Science classes, but I'm not too crazy about History. I like to dance, play volleyball and the guitar. My favourite foods are my mom's brownies and pink lemonade. I really love to shop, watch movies and listen to music when I have a few moments to spare. My pet peeve is people who bite their nails. Yuck! My grandmother's family came to Canada from Ireland. My whole family speaks English and French. I cannot speak Gaelic but maybe someday, when I visit Ireland, I will have the chance to learn a few words.

Bonjou! That is how we say hello in Creole. My name is François and perhaps you guessed that my family comes from Haiti. I speak English, French and a bit of Creole. My grandmother can only speak Creole so I help her communicate with my friends. I love Math and Phys. Ed., but I'm not very good in Art. I play soccer in a league. It's my favourite sport. I also like to play basketball and badminton. I love to watch movies, chat on the Net and hang out with my friends. But don't ask me to go shopping. I really hate that, especially shopping for clothes. My favourite food is cabbage rolls, but I also like pizza, hamburgers and *griot* with fried plantains.

3. Connect with the text.

● Choose the teen you have the most in common with: Marc-Anthony, Virginie, Anna or François.

● Write three things that you have in common and two that make you different. Follow the example.

● See page 24 for helpful language.

4. Go beyond the text.

● Discuss this topic with your class: Does coming from diverse roots make teens very different?

I choose Marc-Anthony. We both speak French. We love soccer. Our favourite food is pizza. Marc-Anthony likes Gym. I prefer Math.....

Helpful
LANGUAGE

In my opinion, …	I think so too.	I think you're right.
I think that …	What do you think?	I disagree.

NOW YOU'RE TALKING

Expressing Preferences, Interests, Tastes and Capabilities

1. Look at the language models.

Expressing preferences

My favourite subject is Math.
We love going to movies.
Football is my favourite sport.
I'm into snowboarding.
I don't like hockey.

I would rather eat chicken.
We both like chicken.
My least favourite is Phys. Ed.
Tommy really hates spiders.
They prefer soccer.

I'm not too crazy about football.
Me neither.
Me too.
Our favourite dessert is fruit salad.

Interests

I like to play hockey.
In my spare time, I read.
We love to shop.
You hate shopping and so do I.

Capabilities

She can speak four languages.
Anna cannot speak Italian.
I'm good at basketball.
I'm not very good in French.

2. Follow along. 🫛 👁

● Listen to Fiona and Shawn talk about themselves.

3. Check it out.

● Look at the conversation on page 25. Find the expressions that Fiona and Shawn use to express preferences, interests and capabilities.

4. Practise.

● Use the expressions on this page and from your notes to tell a partner about yourself.

● Talk about your preferences, your interests and your capabilities.

● Tell your partner where you and your family are from. Complete a double-cell diagram to see what you have in common.

S T R A T E G Y

Pay attention.

• Concentrate on your conversation.

• Listen and respond to your partner.

• Don't be distracted by other conversations.

Shawn: OK, Fiona. You go first.

Fiona: Right. Well, my family and I are from Vancouver, but my ancestors come from Scotland.

Shawn: Most of my ancestors are from China, but I had a grandmother from Ireland. How about sports? What's your favourite?

Fiona: Well, mostly I prefer winter sports.

Shawn: So do I.

Fiona: I love ice-skating. I can skate very well.

Shawn: I'm not a very good skater, but I love to ski. It's my favourite sport.

Fiona: My favourite drink is milk.

Shawn: I prefer apple juice. And I love to eat chicken with barbecue sauce.

Fiona: I like chicken, too, but I would rather eat fish.

Shawn: I don't like fish and I hate seafood. What about school subjects?

Fiona: I really love French, but I'm not too crazy about Math.

Shawn: Me neither. But I love Art.

Fiona: OK then, let's see what is the same and what is different about us.

Shawn: We both love winter sports …

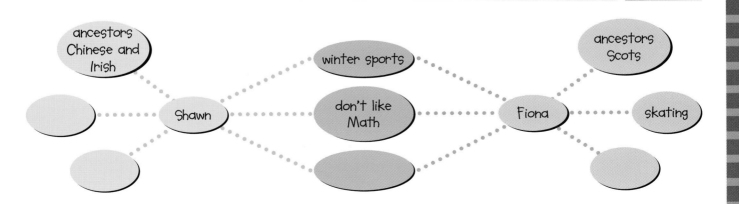

ancestors Chinese and Irish

winter sports

ancestors Scots

Shawn

don't like Math

Fiona

skating

Once Upon a Time

Learning about your roots means discovering interesting stories about your ancestors.

1. Explore the text.

● Work with a teammate.

● Look at the illustrations. What do they say about each story?

● Read Anna's tale, Sarah's story and Tehshang's narrative.

● Use resources to find the meaning of new words.

● Take notes as you read.

Glossary

- starvation = having no food to eat for a long time
- quarantine = imposed period of isolation to prevent spreading disease
- fedora = kind of hat
- fiddle = instrument like a violin
- crowing = sound made by a rooster
- sole = only

S T R A T E G Y

Take notes.

Follow the example to organize the information from each story.

These students learned some unusual facts when they researched their roots.

ANNA'S TALE

My ancestors left Ireland in the mid 1800s. My grandmother's grandfather immigrated to Canada to avoid starvation. That was the time of the Great Irish Potato Famine. Many of the Irish died on the ships crossing over the Atlantic. Others died at Grosse-Isle, near the city of Québec. I guess my great-great-grandfather was very lucky in the end. He survived both the crossing and the quarantine at Grosse-Isle. His son, my great-grandfather Dwyer, was a funny man. He always wore a fedora and he loved to play his fiddle. He played it on his side instead of under his chin. He also made crowing sounds while he played. He was so much fun. He was the sole entertainment at my father's cousin's wedding.

> I wish I had met my great-grandfather. I'm sure he had interesting stories to tell.

Who	Roots	Reason for immigrating	This story is interesting because...	Date
				Mid 1800s
	Ireland	To avoid starvation		

SARAH'S STORY

My mother told me an interesting story about my ancestors. Their names were Éloise and Joseph. Both their families came from France to find work and a new home. My mother said that the couple wanted to get married, but there was no church in their area. So they headed toward the nearest church in a nearby village. On the way, they met a priest who was going down the river in a canoe. Joseph told the priest that he and his girlfriend wanted to get married. The priest was very busy, so he married them right there in his canoe. That was in 1881. My mom says that Éloise and Joseph had 14 children, one of whom was her grandfather.

I think this story is so romantic. How many people do you know who got married in a canoe?

Glossary
- church = house of religion
- headed toward = went in the direction of
- priest = clergyman in Christian churches

2. Respond to the text.

● Which story did you find the most interesting?

● Get into pairs and explain your answer to your partner.

● Use helpful language from pages 23 and 24 to express your opinion.

3. Connect with the text.

● Do you have any stories about your ancestors—parents, grandparents, great-grandparents—to share with your classmates? Get into pairs and exchange tales.

● Look at origins of some common family names in the Culture Pop-Up.

● What is the origin of your family name? Search the Web to find out.

CULTURE POP-UP

Ancestors leave a legacy via family names. From the Irish, we have names such as Browne, Sheridan, Doyle, O'Neill and Kennedy. The Scots gave us names like Armstrong, Campbell, MacDonald, Cook, MacLeod and Johnson. The names Beauregard, Gauthier, Durand, Juneau, Archambault, Tremblay and Lambert are of French origin, while Abbott, Spencer, Johnson and Montague are English.
From the Spanish there is Lopez, Santiago, Torres, Morales, Ruiz and Garcia, while the Germans gave us Schmidt, Boisen, Peters, Mayer and Huber.
This is just a small sample of the many different origins of family names in Québec. Can you name others?

TEHSHANG'S NARRATIVE

GUILLAUME COUTURE

Like many Canadians, I have a very interesting family tree. My mother's family is from China and my father's ancestors are from France. Recently I discovered that I could trace my family roots all the way back to the first settlers in Québec. I was doing a school project on the origins of families when I came across some old family photos and documents.

A long time ago, around the year 1640, a young voyageur from Normandy arrived in Québec. His name was Guillaume Couture. This young man was very talented and quickly learned the language of the natives he traded with. He became an interpreter between the Huron Nation and the French. However, this was a time of war between the Hurons and the Iroquois Nation. Guillaume was captured by the Iroquois. He learned their ways and customs, and they soon adopted him as one of their own. Guillaume played an important role in concluding a peace treaty between the Iroquois and the French. He later married a young French girl by the name of Anne Emard. I also found out that Guillaume Couture has over 50,000 descendants all across North America. There is a statue in his honour as the first settler at Pointe-au-Levis.

I am very proud to have someone in my family who is famous. It makes me feel important but also insignificant compared to my ancestor who was one of the first settlers in Canada. I didn't really care about my roots before, but since my project, I think it is something every teen should try to learn about.

Glossary
• ways = methods, habits

4. Go beyond the text.

● How can you learn about your roots?

● Do you think it is important to learn about your roots?

● Get into teams to discuss and share your conclusions with the class.

5. Extension

● Make a family tree linking as many of your family members as you can.

● Look at the model.

Maxime and Ovelina Spencer
    Lucy Spencer (A.J. Stanutz)   Alice Spencer (George Ruest)
Doris Stanutz (Peter Gauthier)   Spencer Stanutz (Eleonar Dwyer)   Sylvia Stanutz (Arthur St-Jean)   Sheila Stanutz (Guy Daviau)
Linda Gauthier (John Jeffery)   Jo-Ann Gauthier (Robert Boisvert)
Peter Jeffery   Kathleen Boisvert   Jason Boisvert

A Review of the Simple Past

1. Show what you know.

● Choose Anna's tale, Sarah's story or Tehshang's narrative on pages 26–28.

● Make a T-chart in your notebook. List all the verbs in the simple past tense. Organize the verbs into two categories: regular verbs and irregular verbs.

Regular verbs	Irregular verbs
worked	told
	were

2. What the simple past looks like

Affirmative form

- To form the simple past of most **regular verbs**, add **ed** to the **base form** of the verb.
  To want ➠ My ancestors want**ed** a better life.

- When the verb ends in **e**, just add **d**.
  To immigrate ➠ My grandfather immigrate**d** to Canada at the age of ten.

- **Irregular verbs** change form and must be learned. There is a list of irregular verbs on page 176 in the Reference Section.
  To meet ➠ My parents **met** in Europe.
  To leave ➠ My great-grandmother **left** her homeland in 1942.

- Use the same form for all persons.
  Regular verbs   I / you / he / she / it / we / they **played** the fiddle.
  Irregular verbs   I / you / he / she / it / we / they **wrote** letters.

Negative form

- To make a negative statement in the simple past, add **did not** (or the contraction **didn't**) before the base form of all verbs. There is no difference between regular and irregular verbs.
  To want ➠ My great-grandmother **did not want** to move to Canada.
  To know ➠ We **did not know** about our roots.

- Use the same form for all persons.
  I / you / he / she / it / we / they **did not find** any information.

For more information about the simple past, see page 174 in the Reference Section.

➡ Asking questions ⬅

To ask a question, use **did** and the **base form** of the verb. Follow this word order:

Yes/no questions

Did	Subject	Verb	Rest of the question
Did	your ancestors	come	from Europe?
Did	your grandfather	work	on a farm or in a town?

Information questions

Question word	Did	Subject	Verb	Rest of the question
Where	did	your family	come	from?
When	did	your ancestors	arrive	in Canada?
Why	did	they	move	here?

➡ Simple past of the verb *to be* ⬅

Pay special attention to the verb *to be*.

Affirmative form

I / he / she / it **was**   You / we / they **were**

Negative form

Negative form	Contracted version
I / he / she / it **was not**	I / he / she / it **wasn't**
You / we / they **were not**	You / we / they **weren't**

Yes/no questions

Verb	Subject	Rest of question
Was	your grandmother	Irish?
Were	your ancestors	from the Eastern Townships?

Information questions

Question word	Verb	Subject	Rest of the question
Where	**were**	you	born?
When	**were**	your parents	born?

For more information about questions in the simple past, see page 175 in the Reference Section.

3. Practise.

● Work with a partner.

● Prepare three yes/no questions and three information questions about your partner's family history. Look at the charts for examples.

● Take turns asking and answering questions.

30   UNIT 2

End-of-Unit Task

Your Roots

Make a media text to present yourself and one of your ancestors to the class.

1. Plan your work.

● Select a media type to produce. Choose from a poster, video, multimedia computer presentation or suggest an idea to your teacher.

2. Edit your work.

● Share your ideas with a classmate or your teacher to see if they make sense.

● Revise your text and make necessary adjustments to your presentation.

3. Prepare your presentation.

● Practise, practise, practise.

4. Present your media text to the class.

• Choose which family member you want to talk about. It can be a parent, grandparent, great-grandparent. Try to go as far back as possible.

• Include
  – your ancestor's family name and its origin
  – the country, province or city of origin of your ancestor with a map of its location
  – an anecdote or story about your chosen ancestor
  – pictures of your ancestor or illustrations showing the lifestyle he or she led

• Think of what you already know about your family history. Research the information you will need to complete your presentation. Interview family members. Look through old photos. Search the Internet.

• Include any special customs or cultural information you discover about your roots.

• Organize your ideas.

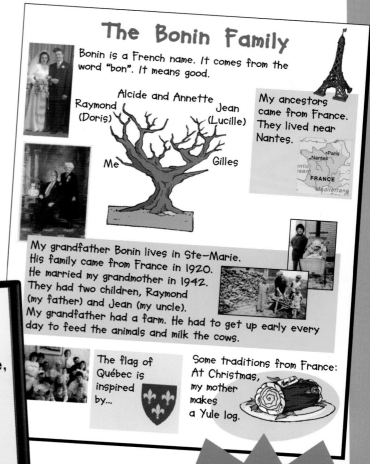

The Bonin Family

Bonin is a French name. It comes from the word "bon". It means good.

Alcide and Annette
Raymond (Doris)   Jean (Lucille)
Me   Gilles

My ancestors came from France. They lived near Nantes.

My grandfather Bonin lives in Ste-Marie. His family came from France in 1920. He married my grandmother in 1942. They had two children, Raymond (my father) and Jean (my uncle). My grandfather had a farm. He had to get up early every day to feed the animals and milk the cows.

The flag of Québec is inspired by...

Some traditions from France: At Christmas, my mother makes a Yule log.

My ancestor, Guillaume Couture, came to Canada in 1640.

GUILLAUME COUTURE

◀◀◀ REWIND

Go through the unit and choose words to add to your vocabulary log.

NOW, THAT'S SCARY!

Your Fear Zone

What are you afraid of?

A. Take this quiz to figure out your fear zone.

- Score 3 points for every time you answered A, 2 points for every B and 1 point for every C.

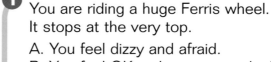

1 You are riding a huge Ferris wheel. It stops at the very top.

A. You feel dizzy and afraid.
B. You feel OK as long as you don't look down.
C. You think the view is great and would like to go even higher.

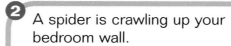

2 A spider is crawling up your bedroom wall.

A. You scream and run away.
B. You take a big shoe and kill it.
C. You take it in your hands and put it outside.

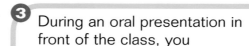

3 During an oral presentation in front of the class, you

A. begin to hyperventilate.
B. sweat and stutter but manage to finish your presentation.
C. give a great presentation. You love the attention.

4 Some friends suggest you go mountain climbing. This idea

A. scares you completely.
B. sounds like fun but only if your best friend goes with you.
C. sounds thrilling. You can't wait to get to the top of the mountain.

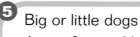

5 Big or little dogs

A. terrify you. You avoid them.
B. make you nervous, but as long as they are with their owner, you're OK.
C. are fun to play with.

Glossary
- crawling up = going up slowly
- nap = short sleep
- silly = ridiculous

6 You and your friends are watching a scary movie.
  A. You go to the washroom every time the music sounds scary.
  B. You hide behind your jacket during the scary scenes.
  C. You watch the movie a second time because it was really fun.

7 During a thunderstorm, you
  A. hide in the basement or in a closet.
  B. jump every time you hear thunder.
  C. take a nap. What else is there to do during a thunderstorm?

8 You think clowns are
  A. scary.
  B. silly.
  C. fun.

What's your fear zone?

Zone 1: 20 points or more
Captain Courageous is not your middle name. Being afraid is no laughing matter. Don't let your fears turn into phobias.

Zone 2: 10 to 19 points
You are prudent, but you still like to have fun.

Zone 3: Under 10 points
Fear is not a problem for you. Be careful: a little fear can help you avoid dangerous situations!

B. On your own, read the following list of scary things. Which do you think are the 10 scariest? Write them in order, 10 being the least scary and 1 the scariest.

- Watching a horror movie
- Spiders, worms or beetles
- Thunder
- Walking in a cemetery
- The dark
- Speaking in front of the class
- Heights
- Flying
- Walking down a dark alley alone
- Halloween
- Crowds
- Death
- Clowns
- Dogs or cats
- The dentist
- Wild animals
- Needles
- Being lost
- Being in a fire
- Deep water

C. Get into teams and make a list of the top five scariest situations.

Helpful LANGUAGE

Giving opinions	Agreeing and disagreeing	
I think spiders are scary.	Me too.	So do I.
In my opinion, clowns are very scary.	I disagree.	I agree.
I think … is/are scarier than …	Not me.	I don't think so.

How Fear Works

How does the body react to scary situations?

1. Look at the body chart.

● List the parts of the body that may show a reaction in a scary situation.

● Find the key words that describe the body's reaction to fear.

Body's reaction to fear:

goosebumps, sweat...

● Compare your answers with a partner.

2. How does your body react to fear?

● Think of a scary situation you experienced in the past, such as going to a haunted house at Halloween, seeing a horror movie or being chased by a dog. How did your body react?

● Write a few notes about the event and how you reacted.

● Share your story with a classmate. Compare your reactions.

Your heart is beating faster. You have goosebumps. You start to sweat. Your face is pale or goes red. You take short, quick breaths, making your mouth dry. Are you in love? Maybe! But, most likely, you are reacting to a scary situation.

Feeling afraid is completely normal. In fact, it is very useful. It makes you cautious and alert. How can fear help you?

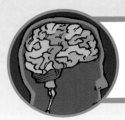

Your brain receives a message that danger is near. It quickly tells your body to get into protection mode.

The pupils of your eyes get bigger. This lets more light into your eyes. It helps you to see better.

You sweat. This helps your body to cool down.

The cooling effect makes your hair stand on end, causing goosebumps. This defence mechanism is great in animals because it makes them look bigger to an attacker. This doesn't work so well with humans.

Helpful LANGUAGE

I noticed that …	First, my heart started to …
I learned that …	Then, I started to …
The text said …	My face was …

Your heart beats faster, sending more blood to your muscles, brain and lungs.

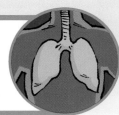

You breathe faster and your airways become wider. This sends more oxygen to the brain so you can think faster.

The blood drains from the surface of your skin and moves toward your vital organs. This helps protect you from blood loss in case of serious cuts. Of course, you become very pale.

Your liver increases the sugar levels in your body to give you an extra boost of energy. Your body releases more adrenaline into your system. This gets you into a "flight or fight" mode, the most basic survival instinct.

So you see, your body is a great machine that can protect you in scary situations.

Glossary
- dry = dehydrated
- drains = empties

When Fear Becomes Phobia

"The only thing we have to fear is fear itself." (Franklin D. Roosevelt)

1. Explore the text.

S T R A T E G Y

Predict.

Look at the title, subtitles, and illustrations. Make a prediction about the text.

● Read the text. Make sure you understand each sentence.

● Use resources to find the meaning of new words.

● Was your prediction right?

2. Respond to the text.

● Use a T-chart to list all the phobias mentioned in the text. Follow the example.

Phobia	fear of
arachnophobia	spiders
chaetophobia	hair

3. Connect with the text.

● Do you know anyone with one of these phobias?

Fear is a natural emotion. It cannot harm you. In fact, it makes you cautious and alert. But for many people, fear can be paralyzing. This is when fear becomes phobia. A phobia is an uncontrollable and usually unreasonable fear of an object or a situation.

Take arachnophobia, for example. Some people start to tremble just looking at a picture of a spider. Arachnophobes know the spider won't actually hurt them. However, something in their brain activates the fear and makes them run away or scream.

Origin of a phobia

Most phobias start with a particular incident that you may or may not remember. Let's say that a dog bit you when you were little. As you grow older, every time you see a dog, you are afraid it might bite you again. The memory of the first incident, consciously or unconsciously, affects the way you feel about dogs. However, just being afraid of dogs does not necessarily mean you have a phobia.

Dealing with phobias

A lot of people with phobias try to avoid their fears. This might be possible if you suffer from alektorophobia (fear of chickens) or hippophobia (fear of horses). You can simply stay away from farms or ranches. But what if you have a fear of sitting down (kathisophobia) or the fear of open spaces (agoraphobia)? It is almost impossible to avoid these situations. In fact, it can be dangerous. One teen who suffered from agoraphobia almost died when his family's house caught fire and he wouldn't leave his room. One way to conquer a fear is to face it. This is not easy to do and you may need the help of a specialist.

Phobia? Really?

Most people with phobias know that their fear is absurd and they often feel embarrassed by it. After all, imagine suffering from auroraphobia (fear of northern lights) or cyclophobia (fear of bicycles). Would you share this information with your friends? Sadly, that doesn't stop the fear from being very real to the person with the phobia. There is a name for just about every fear imaginable. In fact, nomatophobia is the fear of — names! And if some phobias seem sillier than others, remember it is only silly if you are not afraid.

Glossary

- unreasonable = not reasonable
- dealing with = controlling
- caught (fire) = past tense of catch

- share = communicate
- real = true
- sillier = more ridiculous

Do you suffer from didaskaleinophobia (fear of going to school)?

GULP!

Facing Your Fears

1. Look at the language models.

Giving advice	Making suggestions	Asking for advice	Warnings
I would …	Perhaps we could …	How can I …?	Pay attention!
	How about …?	What should I …?	

● A team of students are sharing ideas on how to face their fears.
Pay attention to the words in bold that express advice, suggestions and warnings.

2. Follow along.

1

Mia: I'm afraid of spiders. I really hate them.

Jenny: **You shouldn't be** afraid of spiders. Spiders are very useful.

Mia: Maybe, but every time I see a spider, I just scream.

Alex: **You should try** to face your fear.

Mia: **How can I do that**?

Alex: Well, **we could** find some spiders for you to look at.

Girls: Ah! No!

Shawn: **How about** looking at a picture of a spider?

Jenny: That's an idea.

Mia: No way. I told you I can't even look at spiders.

Shawn: **Why don't you** start by looking at a spider web?

Jenny: Right! Spider webs are pretty to look at. They're actually quite amazing when you think about it.

Mia: I don't know if this is a good idea.

Shawn: Well, you won't know if you don't try.

Alex: Right. **Let's** go outside and try to find a web.

Jenny: Good idea. Come on, Mia, **let's** go.

2

Jenny: See! That wasn't so bad.

Mia: OK, so the spider web was sort of pretty. That doesn't mean I'm comfortable with spiders.

Shawn: **Let's** take a look at this book on bugs. There are cool pictures of spiders in here.

Mia: Um! I'll try.

Alex: Look at this one. It's very colourful. And this one is really tiny.

Mia: Ugh! I think they're ugly. They're creepy.

Shawn: **Maybe we should** go slowly with this. We don't want you to be afraid.

Alex: **You could** take the book home with you and look at it when you're ready.

3. Practise.

● Work with a partner.

● Student A: Tell your partner about a fear you have. Ask for advice. Listen to your partner's advice.

● Student B: Listen to your partner's fear. Give advice. Add a warning.

● Change roles.

S T R A T E G Y

Be cool.

• Don't panic if you have a problem communicating. Take a deep breath and try again.

Dealing With Social Fears

How do you react in a stressful situation?

● Explore the text.

Many people are afraid of doing something that might embarrass or humiliate them in public. These fears include speaking in public, going on stage and speaking a foreign language. Blushing, sweating, dizziness, heart palpitations, trembling and dry mouth are some of the symptoms. Social fears can make people very shy. They try to avoid any situation that makes them uncomfortable.

● Choose three strategies from the list that you think would help you deal with stressful or scary situations.

● Share with the class.

There are ways to deal with social fears, especially when it comes to learning a new language. Here are some helpful tips.

• Ask for help or clarification. Don't think you have to get it right the very first time.

• Ask the speaker to repeat his or her message if you didn't understand what was said. It's normal not to understand everything all the time.

• When trying to express yourself, use gestures if it helps. Many people use their hands to get their message across.

• Stall for time. If someone asks you a question and you're not sure how to answer, say "That's a good question. Let me think about it." Take the time to think of words you already know to give your answer. There is always more than one way to say what has to be said.

• Don't panic and don't become defensive if someone doesn't understand what you said the first time around. Take a deep breath and relax. Stay focused on your task. Use your resources and remember that laughter is the best medicine.

• Don't forget to take risks when trying to communicate. No one will criticize you for your efforts.

• And finally, remember to encourage yourself for a job well done.

Glossary
• going on stage = performing in public
• stay focused = concentrate
• laughter = Ha! Ha! Ha!

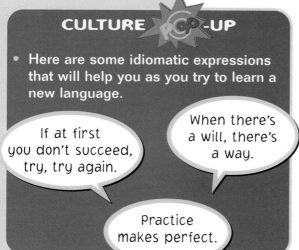

Simple Present or Present Continuous?

1. Show what you know.

● Go back to pages 32 and 33. Find three verbs in the simple present tense. Find three verbs in the present continuous tense. See pages 17 and 18 for help.

> These key words are often used with the simple present tense:
> **usually, sometimes, often, never, every day**

● Work with a classmate and list other key words used with the simple present tense.

> These key words are often used with the present continuous:
> **now, right now, today, this week**

● Work with a classmate and list other key words used with the present continuous tense.

2. When to use the simple present

Use the simple present

- to describe an action that occurs every day, every week, from time to time or to talk about general habits.
  School begins at eight-fifty and finishes at four.
  We often watch horror movies.

- to express a general truth or fact.
  Spiders are not insects.
  Martine plays the clarinet.

- to express likes, dislikes or wants.
  They prefer vegetarian pizza.
  I don't like bugs.
  Josh wants a new CD for his birthday.

- to express a feeling or state that exists in the present.
  We are in Secondary II.
  I feel sick.
  Cats scare me.

For more on the simple present, see page 170 in the Reference Section.

3. When to use the present continuous

Use the present continuous

- to show that a temporary action or activity is in progress now.

  The dog is chasing the squirrel.

  The teacher is talking to Carrie.

  It is snowing.

- to indicate that a temporary action or activity takes place over a period of time.

  Martine is taking clarinet lessons.

  I'm reading the complete volume of the *Lord of the Rings*.

Certain verbs **are not used** in the present continuous.

- Verbs that express feelings or emotions:

to feel	to like	to love
to hate	to need	to want

- Verbs that express a mental attitude or perception:

to forget	to know	to understand
to believe	to seem	

For more on the present continuous, see page 172 in the Reference Section.

I need help
NOW!!!!

 HEADS UP

Don't say	Say
Jake is wanting a glass of water.	Jake wants a glass of water.
I am needing help.	I need help.
OK, I am believing you.	OK, I believe you.

4. Practise.

Simple present or present continuous?

● Complete the sentences using the present continuous or the simple present tense.

● Share your answers with a classmate and explain your choices.

I (*to be*) afraid of the dark and I (*to like, negative*) to be alone. I always (*to imagine*) there is a stranger in the house. It's really dark outside at the moment. It (to rain) very hard. The neighbour's dog (*to bark*) ferociously. This (to make) me nervous right now. I (to tremble) like a leaf. I (*to feel*) very silly but I can't help it. I (*to want*) my mommy!

Fight or Flight

It's time to conquer your fears. Get ready to play a game of Fight or Flight.

1. Before you play the game:

● Form teams and get ready to play.

● Make sure you understand the instructions.

● Go over the language you will need.

• Go to page 38 for helpful language for asking or giving advice, suggestions and warnings.

• See page 42 to check the use of the present continuous.

2. Now play the game.

Game instructions

• You need a game board, a set of game cards, a token (a button or paper clip, for example) and a die to play the game.

• Place your token on the Start square.

• As a team, decide who goes first.

• Roll the die and move your token the number of squares indicated on the die.

• Follow the instructions indicated on the square.

• When you pick a Fight card, read the situation and give appropriate advice. If you cannot give appropriate advice, you must return your token to its previous position.

• When you pick a Flight card, show the illustration on the card to your teammates and describe the situation to them. If you cannot describe the situation correctly or if your teammates do not agree with your description, you must return your token to its previous position.

• The first person to reach the top of Mount Fearless wins the game.

Let's read the instructions first.

STRATEGY

Stall for time.

Use these expressions if you need time to think:

• Wait a minute.

• Let me think ...

• Let's see.

• Well ...

Helpful LANGUAGE

Let's read the instructions first.
Whose turn is it?
What happens if I land on this square?
We have to ...
Let's ask the teacher for help.

◀◀◀ REWIND

Go through the unit and choose words to add to your vocabulary log.

UNIT 4 — SPACE

What Do You Know about Space Travel?

Space travel was just science fiction not so long ago. But after airplane travel became very common, people began to dream about flying to the new frontier, space.

● Work with a partner.

● Decide whether statements 1–6 are true or false.

● Try to come to a consensus.

● Now check your answers by looking through the pages of the unit.

If you got fewer than three answers right, this unit will help you a lot.

Glossary
• fewer = less than

FAST FORWARD ▶▶▶

1 The Americans were the first to send a satellite into space.

2 The Americans were the first to land on the moon.

3 Canadians have never been on a space mission.

4 Astronauts do not brush their teeth while they are in space.

5 Julie Payette is the only Quebecer on the Canadian astronaut team.

6 Canada's most important contribution to the space program is the Canadarm.

Space Travel: A Short History

Get ready to read about the history of space travel.

1. Explore the text with a partner.

● Look over pages 46 and 47. Choose Text A or Text B.

● Pair up with someone who chose the same text.

● Look at the titles, subtitles and photos. What information do they give you?

● Read the text and organize the information in a sequence chart.

● Use resources to find the meaning of new words.

2. Connect with the text.

● What was the most interesting fact for you? For your partner?

Change partners.

● Find a partner who chose the other text.

● Ask each other questions about the texts. Look at the helpful language for ideas.

3. Extension

● Create a newspaper headline to announce the most interesting fact in these texts.

Text A deals with the early years and middle years of space exploration.

Text B talks about recent times.

STRATEGY

Organize information.

Use a sequence chart.

1 Event: first satellite in space (Sputnik 1)

Date:
Who:
Other Information:

2 Event:

Date: 1961
Who:
Other Inform

3 Event:

Date:
Who:
Other Information: first American in space

Period in space history: The early years

5 Event: Apollo missions

Date:
Who:

Helpful LANGUAGE

What was the first important event in the text?
When did it happen?
Who was involved?
What was the most interesting fact for you?

THE EARLY YEARS

Space Travel: The Beginning

1957 marked the dawn of the space age. This was the year the Soviet Union launched the world's first man-made satellite, *Sputnik 1*. *Sputnik 2* also went into orbit the same year, carrying a little dog named Laika. She was the first living creature to orbit the Earth. Yuri Gagarin was the first human to pilot a spacecraft when the Soviet Union launched the *Vostok 1* in 1961.

The Americans sent Alan Shepard into orbit later that same year. The second American to pilot a spacecraft was John Glenn, who orbited the Earth three times in 1962.

Glossary

- dawn = early morning, the beginning
- damaged = caused a malfunction

The Middle Years

Who could put a man on the Moon first? The United States and the Soviet Union started competing in 1963. The Americans won the race six years later when Neil Armstrong, Buzz Aldrin and Michael Collins flew to the Moon in *Apollo 11*. On July 20, 1969, the *Eagle* Lunar Module landed on the Moon's surface.

Armstrong and Aldrin spent three hours walking on the Moon, doing experiments and collecting Moon dirt and rocks. The astronauts also planted an American flag. Collins did more experiments and took photographs while in orbit. The duo spent 22 hours on the Moon before they blasted off back to Earth with Collins.

After *Apollo 11*, there were six more Moon missions between 1969 and 1972. *Apollo 13* was very unlucky: on the way to the Moon, an explosion damaged the craft. The crew survived, but the mission had to be aborted and their return to Earth was very difficult.

IN RECENT TIMES

The most important development in recent times is the space station. These large satellites stay in space for years at a time. The space station is home to different crews of astronauts who take turns living and working there. Astronauts often visit for a few weeks or months. A year is the longest anyone has stayed.

A Lab in the Sky

Skylab was the world's first really big space station. It was launched on May 14, 1973, by the United States. Astronauts came to the *Skylab* to do experiments in space.

They spent over 3000 hours working on board the space station! Spacecraft also used it as an airport. *Skylab* orbited the Earth 2476 times. Three different crews spent a total of 171 days, 15 hours and 14 minutes there. On July 11, 1979, the empty *Skylab* space station re-entered the Earth's atmosphere and burned up over Australia.

Russia's Space Station

The Russians launched the first module of the space station *Mir* in 1986. *Mir* orbited Earth for 15 years. For astronauts from all over the world, it was a home in space. The Russian space station was built from different sections that could be moved around like building blocks. The astronauts could modify the size and shape of the station depending on the needs of different experiments. On March 23, 2001, *Mir* fell into the Pacific Ocean.

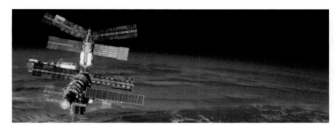

A Space Station for the Future

Sixteen countries worked together to build the *International Space Station* (*ISS*), including Canada, the United States, Russia, Japan, Brazil, and 11 countries from the European Space Agency. Construction began in 1998 and as you read this, the *ISS* is probably still orbiting the Earth. The finished space station will cover the size of a football field (108 metres long). It will weigh 450 metric tons and be the biggest space station ever built. Astronauts can use the *ISS* laboratories to carry out experiments that may lead to better medicines and other important advances. Thanks to the *ISS,* we can also monitor any changes in the Earth's environment and weather around the clock.

Glossary
- monitor = check, record
- around the clock = all the time

Space Culture

Find out about space heroes and their exploits.

1. Look at the photo of the astronauts.

● How many Canadian provinces are represented in the group?

● How many of these astronauts have a doctoral degree?

2. Read about the Canadarm.

● Why are Canadians especially proud of it?

Canadian heroes

Our CSA astronauts are truly talented individuals. They collectively hold more than a dozen academic degrees and have received many honours and professional memberships. Their resumes would impress even the most selective employers. These astronauts had to compete with over 5000 thousand applicants to earn the chance to take astronaut training!

From left to right:
Back row: Col. Chris Hadfield (Ontario), Dr. Dave Williams (Saskatchewan), Dr. Bjarni Tryggvason (British Columbia, born in Iceland)
Front row: Dr. Robert Thirsk (British Columbia), Ms. Julie Payette (Québec), Dr. Steve MacLean (Ontario)

Canadian pride

The Canadarm is a source of pride for all Canadians. Every time the astronauts look out the window of the cabin, the first thing they see is the Canada logo with the red maple leaf on the Canadarm. Canada is the first nation to successfully build a robotic arm. It is used to make repairs on the outside of a spacecraft. The Canadarm is our nation's most recognized scientific achievement.

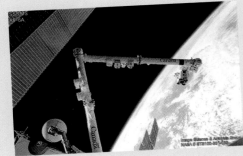

Glossary

- academic degrees = university diplomas
- pride = satisfaction
- achievement = a great accomplishment
- leap = very big step
- mankind = all human beings

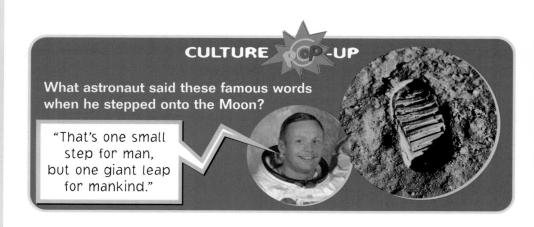

CULTURE POP-UP

What astronaut said these famous words when he stepped onto the Moon?

"That's one small step for man, but one giant leap for mankind."

E-mail from Space

Did you know that astronauts send e-mails to their families and friends?

1. Explore the text.

● Who is this e-mail from?

● When was it written?

● Where was the writer?

2. Respond to the text.

● Use a map to follow Julie Payette's observations from space.

● How long did this part of the trip take?

● Find some words that she uses to express her emotions.

3. Connect with the text.

● What do you know about Julie Payette?

● What do you think of her?

⌧ Hello everyone

Link ▾ Delete Insert ▾

To: `<my friends>`
Cc:
Subject: Hello everyone
▶ Attachments: *none*

Font | Font Size | B *I* U T

Hello everyone.

I'm writing to you from the upper bridge of Discovery after an extraordinary passage over the northern hemisphere. I finally have some free time.

The seventh sunrise of our seventh day in space happened just over the Great Lakes. We passed almost in a straight line along the Saint Lawrence River and, directly below, I saw Montréal at 5:25 a.m. local time on Friday, June 4th, 1999. Soon after it was Québec, then the mouth of the Gaspé, the Chic-Choc mountains, the Îles-de-la Madeleine and Anticosti, with no clouds, all of it magnificent in the rising sun. Incredible!

Only five minutes later, our flight plan took us over Spain, the Straits of Gibraltar, the south of France, Corsica, Sardinia, the Nile River delta and on, and on. All of this in less than 20 minutes! Three of us were madly taking photos in the cockpit, floating from one window to another. It was amazing!!

We thought of the quotation by Leonardo da Vinci which says it all:

"When once you have tasted flight, you will forever walk the earth with your eyes turned skyward, for there you have been and there you always long to return."

Warm greetings to you all.

From space,

Julie

Glossary

• madly = with a lot of energy and enthusiasm

• long to = really want to

The Lighter Side of Space

Time to lighten up! Here is some unusual information about life in space.

- Get into pairs. Choose the most surprising fact on this page and see whether your partner chose the same one.

- Discuss as a class.

Glossary

- lighten up = be less serious
- spit = remove saliva from the mouth
- treadmill = an exercise machine for walking or jogging

- Use the Internet to find out more facts about space travel.

BRUSHING YOUR TEETH IN SPACE

Astronauts do brush in space, almost the same way they do on Earth. They use a regular toothbrush and their favourite toothpaste. But there are no sinks on the space capsule, so they have to spit into a tissue.

SLEEPING IN SPACE

There are no sheets and blankets for the astronauts. They have to sleep in sleeping bags, just like on a camping trip. The bags are attached to the wall of the spacecraft to make sure they don't start floating around during the night.

GOING TO THE BATHROOM IN SPACE

Yes, there are toilets on the spacecraft. But instead of water, there is an air flow, like a vacuum cleaner, to carry the waste from the astronaut's body to a container.

EXERCISING IN SPACE

Astronauts use a treadmill and a rowing machine to exercise in the spacecraft. They need to exercise regularly during the space mission. Otherwise, their bodies start to lose muscle and bone tissue.

WEIGHING YOURSELF ON OTHER PLANETS

It's the pull of the Earth's gravity that decides your weight. But what happens when gravity is different on another planet? Some planets have less gravity than Earth. Would you weigh more or less? Some have more gravity than Earth. What would happen to your weight?

Focus on Form

-ING Words in English

1. Show what you know.

● Look at these examples from the unit. What do you notice about them?
- Brushing your teeth in space
- Sleeping in space
- I'm writing this from the upper bridge.
- Three of us were taking photos.

2. What -ING words look like

- -ING words can be verbs, nouns and adjectives.
  I'm <u>taking</u> Italian lessons.
  <u>Swimming</u> is good for the cardiovascular system.
  I saw a very <u>exciting</u> movie.

- -ING words are formed from verbs. They follow these spelling rules.

- Most verbs add **ing** to the base form of the verb.
  call = call**ing**   study = study**ing**   walk = walk**ing**

- Most short words ending in a consonant double the consonant before adding **ing**.
  plan = plan**ning**   swim = swim**ming**   sit = sit**ting**

- Verbs that end in **e** drop the **e** before adding **ing**.
  take = tak**ing**   give = giv**ing**   write = writ**ing**

3. How to use -ING words

- Use them to form the present and past continuous tenses:
  I **am writing** an e-mail to you.   He **was looking** at the moon.

- Use them as nouns, either in the subject or object position:

  Subject position   Object position
  Eating is necessary for good health.   He is interested in **travelling**.

- Use them as adjectives: He told me a **terrifying** story.

4. Practise.

● Read this paragraph and identify the **-ING** words as nouns, adjectives or verbs.

I am a 14 year-old who loves reading, playing basketball and cooking pasta. This year, I am taking Spanish for the first time. I am hoping to go on a school trip to Mexico. My twin brother is not taking Spanish because he isn't good at learning languages. He is more interested in listening to music. Our parents are going to take us to some concerts this winter. It is going to be an interesting year.

What about You?

Would you like to go on a trip to space?

1. Explore the text.

● Read this text to learn about becoming an astronaut.

● Use all the strategies and resources you need to understand the text.

HOW CAN YOU BECOME AN ASTRONAUT?

According to the Canadian Space Agency, competition for astronaut positions is very intense because so many people are fascinated with the idea of space travel. The candidates who are selected usually have more than one degree in medicine, science or engineering. Some have military training or aviation flight experience. All of them are among the best in their professions. Their common goal is to help improve the quality of life on Earth and in space.

You can improve your chances of becoming an astronaut by:

● Getting at least one advanced degree in science or engineering
● Becoming proficient in more than one discipline
● Developing your public speaking skills, preferably in both official languages (English and French)
● Participating in community activities
● Maintaining your physical fitness
● Learning to skydive, scuba dive or pilot an airplane (optional)

2. Connect with the text.

● Discuss these questions with a partner and then with the whole class.

● Do some research to find out more.

● Are you a candidate for a job in the space industry?
● What are your talents and characteristics?
● What do you need to study? Are you interested in this?
● What else are you good at?
● What can you do now to give yourself a chance to work in the space industry?

Helpful LANGUAGE

I think I could be a candidate. / I don't think I could be a candidate.
I'm good at math (languages, science, etc.).
I'm not good at languages.
I'm good at working with a team.
I'm patient (curious, attentive, etc.).
Well, you need to study math and science.
You could go to space camp.

Glossary

• proficient = competent
• skydive = jump from a plane with a parachute
• scuba diving = swimming underwater with special breathing equipment

Teamwork, Suggestions and Encouragement

1. Look at the language models.

Suggestions	Teamwork and Encouragement
What can we do for this part?	Who wants to do this part?
Let's work together on ...	Would you like to ...?
We could try to ...	Who would like to ...?
We should use the Internet to ...	That's a great idea.

2. Follow along.

Jenny: So, what do we have to do exactly?

Jeff: We have to make up a quiz about fear and phobias for our classmates.

Jenny: But I don't know much about phobias.

Jeff: That's all right. We can use the information in our book.

Jenny: Good idea! Let's start with some easy yes or no questions.

Jeff: Look, there's a lot of information here about the body's reactions to fear. You could write three questions and I could write three. Then we could compare and make sure the questions and answers are all correct.

Jenny: OK, but we should also use the information on phobias on pages 36 and 37.

Jeff: You're right. Let's work together on that, too.

Jenny: OK, and we could also try to find more phobias on the Internet. Then we could create harder questions for our classmates.

Jeff: That's a great idea. Would you like to do that? I can look for information at the library.

Jenny: Fine. Let's start writing some questions now, using the book. Then we can go look for new information.

3. Check it out.

● Find the different ways that Jenny and Jeff make suggestions and give each other encouragement.

4. Try it out.

● Practise the exchange with a partner.

5. Practise.

● Try redoing the conversation by changing the quiz on phobias to a quiz on space travel.

● Use the resources in this unit and the language models on this page.

End-of-Unit Task

Make Up a Space Quiz

Use your question and answer skills to make up a board game.

1. Work with a partner.

● Create game cards for the board game.

● Use resources from this unit and from the Internet or library.

● As you work together, you must use English.

2. Check your work.

● Use resources to check your facts and your language.

3. Make a final version of your cards.

4. Now play the game.

● Form teams of four with other pairs.

● Make sure you understand the instructions.

YOUR GAME CARDS

- You must create 24 questions about space: 12 yes/no questions and 12 information questions.
- Write your questions on 8 cm X 5 cm pieces of cardboard.
- Write the answers in small print at the bottom of the cards.
- Make sure that your questions are correctly formulated. Make sure that the answers are correct, too.
- Put a number at the bottom of each card to show the number of squares a person can move on the game board. Use this number code: hardest questions = 5, easiest questions = 1.
- Your question cards should be clear and easy to read. Keep them together with an elastic band or put them in an envelope.

Game instructions

- You will need a game board, the two sets of game cards prepared by each pair and one token for each pair.
- Place your pile of game cards at your end of the game board.
- Place your token on START.
- As a team, decide who will ask the first question. Pairs must take turns asking a question.
- Pick a card from the top of your pile and read the question to the other pair.
- If they can answer the question correctly, they move their token forward the number of squares shown on the card.
- The first pair to land on FINISH wins the game.

Information question
What was the name of the first satellite to go into space?
Answer: Sputnik 1
(3)

Yes/no question
Do astronauts take showers in space?
Answer: no
(1)

◀◀◀ REWIND

Go through the unit and choose words to add to your vocabulary log.

UNIT 5 — SHOP SMART

Do You Shop Smart?

Time to find out if you are a smart shopper.

- Take this short spending quiz.

- Give yourself one point for every time you answered Yes.

Yes or no?

1. I only buy things I really need.
2. I compare prices before I buy.
3. I wait for sales.
4. I know ads can influence people to buy certain products.
5. I make a budget and stick to it.

> **Your smart shopper profile**
> **4–5** You're a very smart shopper.
> **2–3** You're a good shopper.
> **0–1** You need to examine your shopping habits.

- Do a class survey to find out about your classmates' spending habits.

PROJECT: Make a Shop Smart Guide for Teens

You will produce a guide to help other teens develop their consumer skills.

Remember these things:

- Most teens have money to spend.
- Most of them regularly buy clothes and CDs, and eat out in restaurants.
- Many of them are influenced by the ads they see.
- Many of them need to learn about money management.

Plan your guide:

- Look at the pages in this unit for ideas. Use other resources, too.
- Start collecting ads and other images you could put in your guide.
- Use a planning sheet to guide you.
- Do this project in small groups or on your own.
  Your teacher will help you decide.

FAST FORWARD ▶▶▶

Big Deal: Do the Math

Are all deals necessarily good ones? Check out the following.

● Read what these teens are going to order from the menu.

● Look at the menu and calculate the cost of their meals.

● With a partner, look over the coupons.

● Now calculate the price of the meals with the coupons.

● Which is the best deal?

I think I'll have a Caesar salad, a vegetarian pizza and a cola.

I feel like having spicy fries, the chicken panini and coffee.

Starcos Restaurant
50% off
This coupon gives you 50% off a second meal of equal or greater value.

1 coupon per table

Starcos Restaurant
20% off
on all main courses

1 coupon per table

Starcos Restaurant

∞ Appetizers ∞

Soup of the day	$3.25
Caesar salad	$5.25
Chicken wings (6)	$4.25
Spicy fries	$5.95

∞ Beverages ∞

Coffee, tea, herbal tea	$2.50
Soft drinks	$1.75

∞ Main courses ∞

Pizzas:

All dressed	$8.95
Vegetarian	$7.90

Paninis and Pitas:

Chicken panini	$8.75
Chicken pita	$8.50

Dare to Compare

Make sure you get the best deal. Let's do some comparison shopping.

● Compare the ads for the same product. Which ones are the best deals?

Watch Out!
In an ad, an asterisk (*) usually indicates some special conditions. Beware of the fine print.

PUMP UP THE VOLUME
For the biggest deals in town

Must Haves!
CDs $19 each
Get a second one at 50% off!

BEST HITS
Hottest hits for music lovers! Bargain price: Buy two CDs for $50, get 1 FREE!

#1

GOTTA HAVE IT
Dress to impress!
Brand-names only

Air J sneakers
$130

COPYCAT
Get more for your money
Brand-name, look-alike sneakers* $90

*May have minor imperfections.

● How much will the mountain bike really cost after making all the payments? Do you think this is a good deal?

● Talk about this:
• Which of these products would you buy?
• Do you think a smart shopper always buys the item that is the cheapest?

Mountain High Bike

Get your bike now, pay later! Our best offer: Get our special Mountain High Bike credit card and pay only $30 a month for 48 months. Hurry, because this incredible offer won't last!

$1000

PROJECT ALERT

Find coupons or ads promoting special deals for your guide. Look in magazines, in newspapers and on the Internet. You can also make up the ads yourself. Explain which ad is the best deal and why.

Glossary
• look-alikes = copies

Comparative and Superlative Forms

1. Show what you know.

● Look at the three ads.

● Look at the words in **bold** type in sentences A to D. Which sentences use the comparative form and which use the superlative form?

A. The Hungry Man is **bigger than** the Slim Delight.

B. The Slim Delight is **the smallest** burger.

C. The Hungry Man has **more** beef **than** the Cheese Deluxe.

D. The Cheese Deluxe is **the most** expensive burger.

2. What the comparative and superlative forms look like

➤ Comparative form ◀

Comparisons of equality

To compare two people or things that are similar or equal, use **as** + adjective + **as**.

Tina is **as** tall **as** Brent.   Lemons are **as** sour **as** limes.

Comparisons of superiority or inferiority

To indicate superiority when comparing two people or things, use these forms.

- For short (one-syllable) adjectives, add *er* + **than** to the adjective.
  old = Audrey is old**er than** Tim.

- If a short adjective ends with **e**, just add *r*.
  nice = Annella is nic**er than** Sophie.

- If a short adjective ends with a vowel and a consonant, double the consonant and add *er*.
  big = big**ger than**   hot = hot**ter than**

- If an adjective ends with **y**, change the **y** to **i** and add *er*.
  pretty = Lisa's coat is pretti**er than** Sandra's coat.

- For longer adjectives (two or more syllables), use **more** + adjective + **than**.
  expensive = A car is **more** expensive **than** a bicycle.

To indicate inferiority, use **less** + adjective + **than**.
  This coat is **less** pretty **than** Sandra's but it is **less** expensive, too.

- Do not use **less than** for short (one-syllable) adjectives. Use an antonym instead.
  Don't say: Stacy is ~~less tall than~~ Daniel.   Say: Stacy is short**er than** Daniel.

For more examples, see page 181 in the Reference Section.

Superlative form

To compare **three or more** people or things and indicate superiority, use these forms.

- For short (one-syllable) adjectives, use **the** + adjective + **est**. (If the adjective ends with e, just add **st**.)

  cool = I like the blue jacket and the silver one, but the red one is the cool**est**.

  nice = That backpack is the nice**st** in the store.

- If a one- or two-syllable adjective ends with **y**, change the **y** to **i** and add **est**.

  funny = Kim is the funn**iest** person I know.

- For adjectives of two syllables or more, use **the most** + adjective, or **the least** + adjective.

  expensive = The Cheese Deluxe is **the most** expensive burger.

  The Slim Delight is **the least** expensive.

For more examples, see page 181 in the Reference Section.

3. Practise.

- Go back to page 57.

- Check out the ads to find adjectives in the superlative form.

- Now work in pairs. Look at the following ads.

- Take turns comparing the cars that are advertised.

Some adjectives have irregular comparative and superlative forms.

good ➠ better than ➠ the best

bad ➠ worse than ➠ the worst

much/many ➠ more than ➠ the most

far ➠ farther than ➠ the farthest

The Vroomette
$10,000
compact

The Gooddeal
$18,000
environmentally friendly

The BIG BOSS
$90,000
classy

PROJECT ALERT

Use the comparative form in your guide when comparing deals and sale items. Use the superlative form to create catchy ad titles for your guide.

Ads That Work

Advertisers use different techniques to get us to buy their products.

- Explore this article.

- Find the name of the advertising techniques mentioned in the text.

- Work with a partner. Look at the ads on page 61.

- Identify the marketing strategies and advertising techniques that are used.

- What makes each of these ads attractive to teens?

- Slogans are also part of the marketing strategies that work. Scan the ads on page 61 and find the slogans that are used.

- Which ads have the catchiest slogans? Why?

Glossary

- beverages = drinks
- nerds = foolish, uninteresting people
- improved = made better
- stand-by = proven technique

ADVERTISING TECHNIQUES

Ads are everywhere! You see them on TV, in bus shelters, on food packaging, on billboards, on the Internet, in magazines and even in public bathrooms. Advertisers use innovative methods to try to sell us products. Often they try to sell us an image of what we could be like if we bought the product. To be a smart consumer, it is important to know the techniques companies use to make us spend our money.

Tricks of the trade

- The "ideal family" technique uses the image of the perfect family to sell products. Every family member in these ads looks great and wears cool clothes. This image represents what we wish our own family could be like: happy, attractive, and harmonious.

- The "instant excitement" trick is often used to sell food or beverages. We see people eating or drinking certain products. Just a bite or a sip and they're suddenly riding a giant rollercoaster or mountain biking down a steep hill. Wouldn't we like to have that much fun, too?

- The "just for cool people" marketing technique sends the message that using a particular brand will turn us into cool kids. It's our chance to finally join the cool crowd! The ads try to convince us that only nerds would ignore such a hot product.

- The "star power" approach uses celebrities to sell goods of all kinds. Advertisers know that when we see our favourite star or athlete using a product, the message we get is that it must be the best thing on the market.

- And let's not forget that old advertising stand-by, using catchy words like *NEW, SPECIAL, WONDERFUL, NATURAL*, etc. These words make us believe that what we already have just isn't good enough anymore. So we need to buy these new, improved versions.

What can we do about it?

Be a smart consumer. Learn the difference between buying something because you're influenced by an ad and buying something you really need. Keep in mind that ads exist to influence us into buying the products they promote.

TIGER Power Bar

The TIGER shows no mercy! Because there's nothing you'd like better than to outrun the competition, we created the Tiger sport high-energy bar. The ultimate energy food, Tiger Power Bars! Available at fine health food stores.

Orange Blast!

The natural way to start your day! Just one cup equals two servings of fruit. A healthy diet rich in a variety of fruit may help reduce the risk of some types of cancers.

MINTY WILD candies

Get the cool fresh taste of winter in your mouth! MINTY WILD

ZITS AWAY
Power over pimples.

Having acne is no fun at all, especially when the products you try aren't working. Fortunately, there's a NEW acne medicine that can give you the positive results you're looking for.

Get clear, clean-looking skin.

Glossary
- outrun = run faster than
- zits = pimples

PROJECT ALERT

- Use resources to find an ad you like for your guide.
- Highlight the slogan and underline the catchy words.
- Name the advertising technique that is used.
- Write a few sentences to show how the technique tries to convince people to buy that product.

Strategies for Smart Shopping

What can you do to be a smart shopper?

● Read what these teens are saying.

● Find their rules for smart shopping.

● Talk about this with a partner: Which of these rules do you follow?

Teen 1: Jasmine

I don't want to spend a fortune on a nice pair of jeans. That's why I shop around to compare prices. This way, I'm sure to get the best deal for my money.

Teen 2: Nelson

I'm into electronics. When I shop, it's important for me to ask questions about the guarantee and the type of after sale service plan the store offers.

Teen 3: Misha

I hate buying under pressure. I avoid shops where the clerk makes me feel like I absolutely have to buy something I don't need.

Teen 4: Debbie

I love to shop for clothes. I try not to be influenced by specials that are too good to be true. I take the time to think before I buy an item and I stay within my budget.

PROJECT ALERT

You could include these rules in your guide and find other rules to help teens become better shoppers.

Money Management Tips

Making a budget (and sticking to it!) is a good thing to do if you want to spend your money wisely.

- Look at David's financial situation.

- How much money does David receive every month? And how much does he spend?

- Does he have good money management skills?

This is David's income.

David gets an allowance of $35 a week. He also walks the neighbour's dog every Saturday and makes $5 for each walk. Twice a month, he babysits for his aunt and makes $12 each time. David is responsible for buying food and snacks, for his entertainment and transportation.

This is David's monthly spending budget.

Monthly Expenses	Amount budgeted
Hobbies	$40
Movies	$30
Food, drinks, snacks	$25
Transportation (bus fare)	$25
Video games	$20
Other	$20
Magazines	$10

- What about you? What are your spending habits?

- Answer these questions.

1. How much allowance do you get every week?
2. Do you have any other income?
3. How much money do you spend on
   - food and drinks?
   - entertainment (movies, CD's, video games, magazines, etc.)?
   - clothes?
   - personal care items (make-up, hair products, etc.)?
4. Do you sometimes have to borrow money from your parents or your friends?
5. Do you have any savings?

PROJECT ALERT

You could include a section on budgets in your guide.

Giving and Asking for Advice

1. Look at the language models.

Giving advice	Asking for advice
You could make a budget.	Should I buy this sweater now?
You should read the ads closely.	Do you think this is a good deal?
I think you should compare products.	Is this a real bargain?
You should do the math.	What do you think?
Maybe you could ...	What should I do?

2. Check it out.

● Look at the conversation on page 65.

● Find the words that Shawn and Alex use to give advice and to ask for advice.

3. Follow along.

● Shawn and Alex are looking at an ad for CDs. Listen to their conversation.

4. Practise.

● Work with a partner.

● Use the expressions on this page to give or ask for advice. Talk about this:

- Ask for your partner's advice about buying certain brand name products (jeans, shoes, etc.).
- Give advice on buying these products.
- Ask for your partner's advice about a product in an advertisement you saw (shampoo, makeup, video games, etc.).
- Give advice on the product and/or on the advertisement.

STRATEGY

Practise.

If you have difficulty with this exercise, repeat the activity with new products or ads. Practising really does help.

HEADS UP

You can use the imperative form to give orders and advice.

- Be a smart shopper.
- Wait for sales!
- Don't waste your money!
- Compare before you buy.
- Wait until you have the money.

Alex:	Did you see the ad about the Pump Up CD super sale?
Shawn:	Yes, I did.
Alex:	Do you think it's a good deal?
Shawn:	I don't know. I think you should do the math and compare prices with another store.
Alex:	I'm also thinking of buying the four CDs I want while they're on sale. What do you think?
Shawn:	Do you have enough money for that?
Alex:	Well, I have $20. Could you lend me another $20?
Shawn:	No way! Every week it's the same story. You really should learn to manage your money more wisely. You could start by making a budget.
Alex:	You're right. I never have enough money to last a whole week. Maybe you could teach me when I get my next allowance?
Shawn:	No problem. You could start immediately by putting the $20 you already have in a bank account.
Alex:	And miss out on the best sale of the year?!!

<img_1: PROJECT ALERT>

Your Shop Smart Guide

It's time to decide what you will put in your guide.
By now you have seen many elements that could appear in it.

UNIT 5

Your Shop Smart Guide

PROJECT: Make a Shop Smart Guide for Teens

Pull it all together.

- You can set up your guide as an information booklet or a multimedia computer presentation, or suggest another idea to your teacher.

- Make a cover page and give your guide a catchy title.

- Include elements from the following categories:
  - comparing ads to find the best deals
  - examples of techniques used by advertisers
  - rules to become better shoppers
  - and some money management tips

- Give at least one example of smart shopping advice on each page.

- Make a sketch of each page of your guide. Write a first draft of the texts and correct them.

- Make a final version with cut-out pictures and drawings. If you can, use a computer to make your guide attractive and easy to read.

- Go over the checklist to make sure you have done everything.

Go public.

- Display all the guides and decide as a class who has the best presentation and gives the most useful tips.

ADD IT UP!

T-shirts
Buy one at $20, get another 25% off!

T-shirts
Buy two for $30, get one FREE!

- Do the math before you decide to buy.
- Calculate the price of a single shirt to see if you're getting a good deal.
- You should ask yourself: Do I really need three new T-shirts?

WATCH OUT!

Pearly Whites
The NEW way to get a brighter smile!

PEARLY WHITES

- Don't believe everything you see in ads.
- Know the advertising techniques that are used. This ad uses the "for cool people only" marketing technique and catchy words.

◀◀◀ REWIND

Go through the unit an choose words to add t your vocabulary log.

FROM TIME TO TIME

As Time Goes By

What do you know about these historical events?

A. Match the events and the dates on the timeline.

● Get in pairs to discuss your answers. Try to arrive at a consensus.

● Look at the Helpful Language box for useful expressions.

B. Personalize the timeline.

● Add these dates to a timeline:
  • your year of birth
  • your mother's year of birth
  • the year you will finish secondary school

● Tell your partner what your additions are.

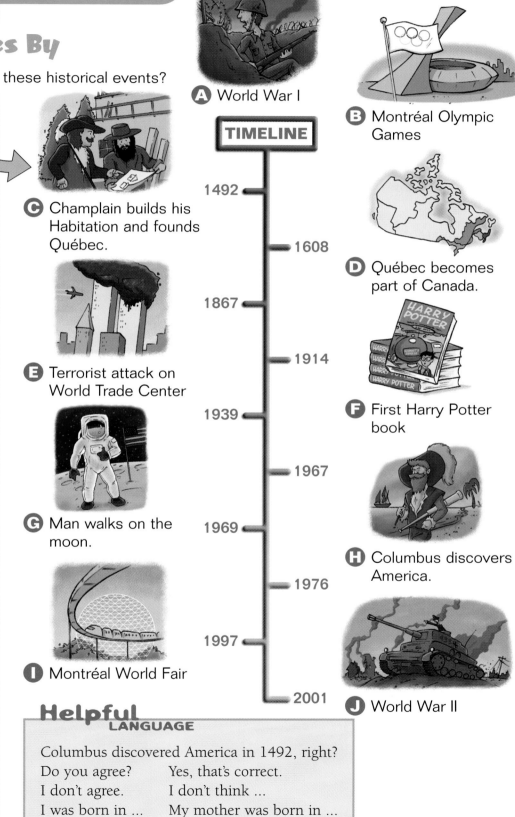

A World War I

TIMELINE

1492

1608

1867

1914

1939

1967

1969

1976

1997

2001

B Montréal Olympic Games

C Champlain builds his Habitation and founds Québec.

D Québec becomes part of Canada.

E Terrorist attack on World Trade Center

F First Harry Potter book

G Man walks on the moon.

H Columbus discovers America.

I Montréal World Fair

J World War II

Helpful LANGUAGE

Columbus discovered America in 1492, right?
Do you agree?   Yes, that's correct.
I don't agree.   I don't think ...
I was born in ...   My mother was born in ...

Travelling in Time

History is all about the past, the present and the future.

1. Explore the text.

S T R A T E G Y

Skim and scan.

- Skim to get a general idea of the text.
- Scan to find specific information.

● On your own, look at pages 69–73.

● What is the story about?

● What are the three main time periods in the story?

● Which dates are mentioned?

● Compare your answers with a partner.

● If you disagree on some answers, scan the story again to see what it says.

2. Follow along.

● Read the story as you listen to the recording.

Hi, my name is Simon Leblanc. This is my friend Kim Lee. We are going to travel in time. So, come on and join us.

CULTURE POP-UP

It's about time.

This unit contains many expressions about time.
- Scan through the story to find idiomatic expressions with the word *time*.
- Can you guess their meaning?

PART 2

Look. What's happening?! The present is disappearing!

Oh, wow! That's old Québec.

3 SIMON AND KIM NOW SEE TWO YOUNG PEOPLE, JACQUES LEMOYNE AND KATHLEEN O'BRIEN, LIVING IN QUÉBEC CITY IN THE YEAR 1853. THEY HAVE JUST MET, SO THEY TELL EACH OTHER ABOUT THEIR LIVES. JACQUES WAS BORN IN QUÉBEC. KATHLEEN CAME FROM IRELAND. JACQUES GOES TO COLLEGE AND WANTS TO BE A LAWYER. KATHLEEN DOESN'T GO TO SCHOOL BECAUSE SHE HAS TO HELP WITH THE YOUNGER CHILDREN AT HOME.

4 THEY TALK ABOUT THE HARD TIMES. WHEN KATHLEEN CAME FROM IRELAND, IT TOOK SEVERAL WEEKS TO CROSS THE OCEAN BY SHIP. THEY WERE IN QUARANTINE ON GROSSE-ÎLE FOR A MONTH. MANY FRIENDS DIED OF CHOLERA ON THIS ISLAND. LIFE WAS HARD FOR JACQUES' FAMILY, TOO. JACQUES' GRANDMOTHER DIED FROM INFLUENZA DURING LAST YEAR'S EXTREMELY COLD WINTER.

5 BUT NOW IT IS SUMMER. THE WEATHER IS WARM AND SCHOOL IS OVER. JACQUES INVITES KATHLEEN TO THE JUNE 24 CELEBRATIONS.

3. Respond to the text.

● These are the events of Simon and Kim's story. Put them in chronological order on a timeline.

● Follow this model.

Past (1853)	1.	F
	2.	
	3.	
Present	4.	G
	5.	
	6.	
	7.	
Future (2050)	8.	J
	9	
	10.	

4. Connect with the text.

● Which time period would you prefer to live in, 1853 or 2050? Why?

● Share your ideas with your classmates.

5. Extension

● Imagine Québec in the year 3000. What do you think it will be like?

A Kim types the date *September 20, 2050*.

B Jacques asks Kathleen to go to the Saint-Jean parade with him.

C Kim asks Simon what time it is.

D Greg offers to do a multimedia presentation for the project.

E Simon shows Kim how the time travel program works.

F Kathleen tells Jacques about the quarantine on Grosse-Île.

G Simon invites Kim to his house after school.

H Greg, Anna, Maxime, Jade and Matt talk about their roots.

I Jacques and Kathleen sing around a bonfire.

J The teacher assigns a group project about ancestors.

Helpful LANGUAGE

I think that ...

I don't think that ...

I prefer ... because ...

I predict that Québec will be ...

The Future Tenses

1. Show what you know.

● Go back to the story on pages 69 to 73.

● Find two examples of verbs in these tenses: past, present, future.

2. What the future tenses look like

➡ The Future Simple ⬅

Affirmative form

- To form the future simple, use **will** (or the contraction **'ll**) with the base form of the verb.
- Use the same form for all persons.

I **will eat** lunch in the cafeteria at noon.
You **will travel** to the moon someday.
He **will enjoy** the movie.
We **will have** a new teacher next class.
They **will go** to the hockey game.

I**'ll eat** with my friends.
You**'ll travel** by spaceship.
She**'ll enjoy** it, too.
We**'ll have** to be on time.
They**'ll go** by bus.

Negative form

- Use **will not** (or the contraction **won't**) with the base form of the verb for all persons.

I **will not eat** lunch in the cafeteria today.
He **will not enjoy** the movie.
They **will not go** to the hockey game.

I **won't eat** with my friends.
She **won't** enjoy it either.
They **won't go** by bus.

Yes/no questions

- Use **will** + subject + base form of the verb for all persons.

Will you **travel** to the moon someday?
Will he **enjoy** the movie?
Will they **take** the bus?

Information questions

- Place the question word first.
When **will** you **travel** to the moon?
Who **will teach** our English class?
What **will** we **discover**?
How **will** they **get** there?

For more on the future simple, see page 178 in the Reference Section.

➡ The Future with *going to* ⬅

To form the future with *going to*, use the verb *to be* + *going to* + the base form of the verb.

Affirmative form	With contracted form of *to be*
I **am going to study** with my friend. (intention)	I'm going to study.
You **are going to like** the dessert. (prediction)	You're going to like it.
He **is going to watch** TV. (prediction)	He's going to watch.
We **are going to listen** to music. (intention)	We're going to listen.
They **are going to play** video games. (prediction)	They're going to play.

For more on the future with going to, see page 179 in the Reference Section.

3. When to use them

The future with **going to** is often used to talk about an intention or make a prediction.

The future with **will** is generally used to talk about a probable future action or situation.

These time markers are often used with the future tenses: *soon, later, tonight, tomorrow, on Saturday (Sunday, Monday, Tuesday, etc.), next week, next month, next year.*

4. Practise.

What are your plans for the weekend?

● Write five statements about your weekend activities. Use **will** and **going to**.

● Tell your partner about your weekend plans.

Suggestions for actions

read a book

play the drums

go to the shopping mall

make pizza

phone friends

sleep until noon

dance a lot

eat lasagna

Talking about Future Plans

1. Look at the language model.

● Alex and Jenny are talking about their plans. Pay attention to the words in **bold** that express statements and questions about the future.

2. Follow along.

> **What are you going to do** this weekend?

> I'm not sure. I have no plans right now.

> **There's going to be** a concert at the arena on Saturday.

> Great! **Who's going to play**?

> **There will be** a group from Montréal called the K-Tones, and a singer from Sherbrooke.

> **Will you go** on your own?

> Well ... What do you mean?

> I mean ... We could go together.

> OK. **I'll meet you** at the front door.

> Right. **I'll be there** at eight o'clock.

3. Practise.

● Work with a partner.

● Choose one of these events or make one up.
- rap concert
- talent contest
- pizza party
- fashion show
- movie

● Do a role-playing activity using the above model.

STRATEGY

Use resources.

- Use resources to prepare for oral interaction. It will give you confidence.

- Look for the vocabulary and expressions you will need beforehand.

- Check your verb tenses.

End-of-Unit Task

Timeline of Your Life

Make a timeline of your life.

1. Choose events in the past, present and future.

- Past: birth, primary school, pets
- Present: Secondary II, hobbies, friends
- Future: end of secondary school, future studies, jobs, personal projects

2. Make a timeline poster.

● Place each event on a timeline.

● Write a sentence for each event.

STRATEGY

Use resources.

- Use resources for all your writing projects.
- Look at the model for ideas.
- Check your verb tenses. Look in the Reference Section.

● Have a classmate check your work.

● Add photos or pictures of yourself and of special events.

4. Present your timeline to your classmates.

◀◀◀ REWIND

Year of event	Description of event
1993	I was born in Granby on May 12.
1995	We moved to Victoriaville.
1998	I was in Grade 1.
2004	I took guitar lessons.
2006	I am in Secondary II. My best friend's name is Brandon.
2007	I will be fifteen years old.
2008	I will get my driver's licence.
2009	I will graduate from secondary school.
2011	I will be a car mechanic.

HEADS UP

- For past events, use the past tense: *I was born in ... I went to ...*
- For present events, use the present tense: *I am ... I have ...*
- For future events, use **will** and **going to**: *I will go to ... I am going to study ...*

Go through the unit and choose words to add to your vocabulary log.

BODY MECHANICS

Getting Active

Everyone knows about the importance of being active in order to keep healthy.

How active are you?

A. Look at the activities on this page.

● Which ones do you do? How often?

● Which ones would you like to try?

● What other activities can you do to get fit?

B. Form pairs.

● Tell your partner how you feel about each of the activities on this page.

● Find out if your partner agrees.

jogging

cycling / biking

in-line skating

swimming

team sports

walking

yoga

skateboarding

skating

Helpful LANGUAGE

I go swimming twice a week.
I cycle every day in the summer.
I go skating often in the winter.
I do yoga every week.
I play soccer in the spring.
I want to try a team sport.
I can go snowboarding.
I could take a dance class.

I hate jogging but I love cycling.

Well, I really like jogging. I enjoy cycling, too.

I like to play hockey. It's really fun.

I agree. I like it, too. But soccer is my favourite sport.

Health: What's It All About?

The World Health Organization describes health as a state of complete physical, social and mental well-being and not just the absence of disease.

- Find out if these two teens are healthy.

- Form pairs. Decide who will read Tim's profile and who will read Amy's.

- Use a T-chart to organize the information in each text.

Good habits	Bad habits

- Share your findings for Tim and Amy.

- Decide who is the healthiest.

STRATEGY

Make an intelligent guess.

- Think about the information you found for each category.

- Make an intelligent guess to decide if the person is healthy or not.

- What advice would you give them?

Glossary
- obsession = a way of acting or thinking that you cannot stop

Tim's Profile

Tim is a Secondary III student. Since about the age of 10, Tim has been almost obsessive about some foods. He cuts off any pieces of fat on meat. He always checks the dates on food items. If it is even one day past the date, he will not eat them. He washes all his fruit with soap and water to get rid of pesticides. But he loves sugar! Every day, he stops at the corner store and buys a couple of chocolate bars or another kind of candy.

Tim started smoking this year even though he knows this is pretty stupid. He works out nearly every day, either by lifting weights at home or by jogging around the track at the park. Even on freezing cold days, you can see Tim running around the neighbourhood.

Amy's Profile

Amy began to gain weight when she was 12 years old. She was very worried because the message she got all the time was "Thin is in!" She tried many diets but they never worked. She always ended up putting on the weight she had lost, sometimes even more. Finally Amy agreed to see a doctor and a nutritionist who gave her some good advice about healthy lifestyles. She decided to stop her obsession with weight. Now, she is almost a vegetarian but she eats fish. From time to time, she gives herself a special treat like ice cream, fries or a milkshake.

Amy doesn't like exercising very much, however. Everyone says she should do something, but she hasn't found a good activity yet.

Get Moving

Find out what Health Canada has to say about activity and health.

1. Look at the cover page of this Health Canada document.

● What is the title of the document?

● Who was involved in producing this document?

● What activities are featured on this cover?

● Predict what the document is about. Write down one or two ideas you have.

S T R A T E G Y

Predict.

What elements on the cover tell you what the full document is about?

● Now turn the page and check your predictions.

CANADA'S
Physical Activity Guide
to Healthy Active Living

Canada's Physical
Activity Guide
for Youth

Physical activity is Fun!
At home
At school
Inside or outside
On the way to and from school
With family and friends

Adding more physical activity to your day
equals better health, strength and well-being!

Health Canada   Santé Canada

The College of Family Physicians of Canada

Canadian Paediatric Society

CSEP SCPE Canadian Society for Exercise Physiology

2. Check your predictions.

● Skim the text to see if you predicted correctly. Don't look at anything else for the moment.

3. Explore the text.

● Look at the four sections of the document.

● Read the information in each section and make sure you understand it.

● Remember to use strategies and resources.

● For each section:
  • write down the most important points.
  • make a personal statement about what you think of each point.

● You can use a reading log to record your answers.

● Compare answers with a partner.

Glossary
• throughout = during
• make you breathe deeper = force you to breathe deeper
• instead of = in place of

---

section 1

Dare to be Active!

Tune into physical activity to:

• Meet new friends
• Improve physical self-esteem
• Achieve a healthy weight
• Build strong bones and strengthen muscles
• Maintain flexibility

• Promote good posture and balance
• Improve fitness
• Strengthen the heart
• Increase relaxation
• Promote healthy growth and developme[nt]

Let's Get ACTIVE!
Canada's Guidelines for INCREASING Physical Activity in Youth

This Guide will help you:

1. INCREASE time **CURRENTLY** spent on physical activity, starting with 30 minutes **MORE** per day (See CHART BELOW)

2. REDUCE "non active" time spent on TV, video, computer games and surfing the Internet, startin[g] with 30 minutes **LESS** per day (See CHART BEL[OW])

Build up physical activity throughout the day in periods of at least 5 to 10 minutes

MONTH	Daily INCREASE in moderate* activity (Minutes)		Daily INCREASE in vigorous** activity(Minutes)		Total Daily INCREASE in physical activity (Minutes)	Daily DECREASE in non-active time (Minutes)
Month 1	at least 20	+	10	=	30	30
Month 2	at least 30	+	15	=	45	45
Month 3	at least 40	+	20	=	60	60
Month 4	at least 50	+	25	=	75	75
Month 5	at least 60	+	30	=	90	90

Congratulations!
Daily active time is part of a healthy lifestyle.

*Moderate physical activity examples
• Brisk walking, skating, bike riding

**Vigorous physical activity examples
• Running, supervised weight training, basketball, soccer

section 2

Here's the scoop!

— Combine three types of physical activity for best results:

1. **Endurance** activities that make you breathe deeper, your heart beat faster, and make you feel warm.

2. **Flexibility** activities like bending, stretching and reaching that keep your joints moving.

3. **Strength** activities that build your muscles and bones.

Here are some ideas to get you started

Decide to take the first step – It's all up to you – And YOU can DO it!

- Walk more – to school, to the mall, to the park, to your friend's house

- Walk, run or bike instead of getting a drive with mom or dad

- Take the dog for a walk

- Run, jump, skateboard, snow-board, ski, skate or toboggan

- Play sports

- Go skating, swimming, bike riding or bowling

- Rake the leaves, shovel snow or carry the groceries

- Take a class like yoga, hip hop, aerobics or gymnastics

- Check out some activities at the community centre

- Be active with your friends

- Put on some music and move

- Stretch your muscles every day

- Try something new like wall climbing or dance classes

Choose activities you like or think you might like.

More on Modals

1. Show what you know.

I think Tim should stop smoking. He must know that it's bad for his health. I'm sure he can do it. Amy should try yoga. She might like it. Or she could play volleyball with her friends.

● Look at Malika's speech balloon. Can you identify the modal verb in each sentence?

● What meaning does each one indicate? Choose from the following list:

- obligation or necessity
- possibility
- permission
- ability or capacity
- suggestion or advice

2. What modals look like and when to use them

CAN / CAN'T

- CAN indicates an **ability** or **capacity** to do something.
  James can speak Spanish.
  I can meet you at the gym.

- CAN'T (or CANNOT) indicates an **inability** or **incapacity** to do something.
  They can't play tennis very well.
  Priya is sick today, so she can't go to school.

CAN / MAY

- Use CAN or MAY to ask for **permission**, and to give permission or refuse it. MAY is more formal than CAN.
  May I go to the washroom?   Yes, you may.   No, you may not.
  Can I go jogging with you?   Yes, you can.   No, you can't.

MAY / MIGHT / COULD

- Use MAY, MIGHT or COULD to indicate a **possibility**.
  It may snow tonight.
  Sarah might try yoga this fall.
  We could check the facts on the Internet if we're not sure.

- Use MAY, MIGHT or COULD to answer a question **when you are not sure**.
  Q: Will it rain tomorrow? A: It may rain. I'm not sure.
  Q: Are you going to participate in the debate? A: I might. I'm thinking about it.
  Q: What sport should Mel try? A: Well, she could try swimming or cycling.

SHOULD / SHOULDN'T

- Use SHOULD or SHOULDN'T to make a **suggestion** or to give **advice**.
  You should play soccer with us this year.
  We shouldn't eat so much junk food.

MUST / HAVE TO

- Use MUST or HAVE TO to indicate an **obligation** or a **necessity**.
  You must pay attention in class.

- Use MUST + NOT (MUSTN'T) to indicate an **obligation** or something that is **not permitted**.
  You mustn't chew gum in class. That's the rule.

- Use DO NOT HAVE TO to indicate that there is **no obligation or need** to do something.
  The History test was cancelled. You don't have to study tonight.
  Mila eats well. She doesn't have to go on a diet.

WOULD

- Use WOULD LIKE TO to express **a wish or desire**.
  I would like to visit Greece.
  We'd like to go snowboarding.

- Use WOULD RATHER to express a **preference**.
  I would rather play basketball than go swimming.
  I think he would rather take judo lessons.

3. Practise.

● First, make a chart like this in your notebook.

Ability or capacity	Possibility	Suggestion or advice	Obligation or necessity	Wish or desire
	I might get a new computer.			

● Write a complete sentence for each category in the chart, using the correct modals. Choose an action from the box below that works with each modal. Look at the example in the chart.

be late	speak English in English class	get a new computer	eat only chocolate
sing well	take a shower every day	cheat on a test	exercise every day

● Check and compare your answers with a partner.

What Should I Do?

NOW YOU'RE TALKING

1. Follow along.

● Listen to Mia and Jeff's conversation.

Mia: My parents say I should do more physical activities. But I don't really like sports. What should I do?

Jeff: Well, you might try talking to the Phys. Ed. teacher.

Mia: Right, I could do that. What about you? Do you play a lot of sports?

Jeff: Yeah, I do. I play hockey in the winter and baseball in the summer. You don't have to do team sports, though. But you really should do something.

Mia: Like what?

Jeff: Well, you could try activities like judo or karate. You should try one of those to see if you like it.

Mia: Good idea. What else could I do?

Jeff: Hmm. You could always just go for long walks.

Mia: Like with my dog, right?

Jeff: Right!

2. Check it out.

● Find the different ways that Jeff gives suggestions and advice to Mia. What do you notice about the verbs in these sentences?

3. Practise.

● Work with a partner.

● Decide who has Situation 1 and Situation 2 below. Think about the situations. Take notes.

● Think of a short conversation for each one and act it out.

● Use modal verbs to ask for and give advice. You can look at Mia and Jeff's conversation for ideas.

STRATEGY

Say it differently.

To make sure you understand, you can repeat what your partner said using different words.

Example:
You could always try jogging.
You mean, I should go for a run?

Situation 1
You love playing hockey but you hate getting up early in the morning for practice. Explain your situation and ask your partner for some advice.

Situation 2
You love sports like basketball and volleyball. But you are not very tall or strong. Explain your situation and ask your partner for some advice.

The Buddy Column

The Buddy Column is an advice column. People write to Buddy and explain their problems.

Buddy received these two e-mails this week. Help him out.

1. Write an e-mail back to one of the teens.

● Give Sebastian or Arianne some advice.

● Your e-mail should include:
  • At least four sentences
  • At least two modal verbs

● Use the writing process and resources.

2. Check your work.

● Your e-mail should be clearly written. Use a computer if possible.

● Exchange e-mails with a partner. Help each other to improve them.

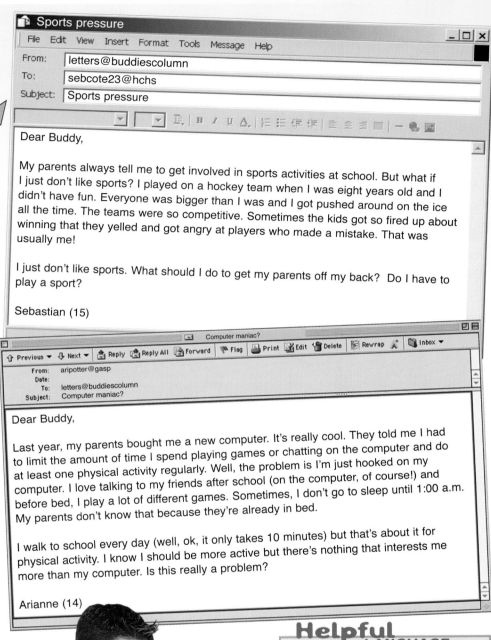

Sports pressure

File   Edit   View   Insert   Format   Tools   Message   Help

From: letters@buddiescolumn
To: sebcote23@hchs
Subject: Sports pressure

Dear Buddy,

My parents always tell me to get involved in sports activities at school. But what if I just don't like sports? I played on a hockey team when I was eight years old and I didn't have fun. Everyone was bigger than I was and I got pushed around on the ice all the time. The teams were so competitive. Sometimes the kids got so fired up about winning that they yelled and got angry at players who made a mistake. That was usually me!

I just don't like sports. What should I do to get my parents off my back? Do I have to play a sport?

Sebastian (15)

Computer maniac?

⇧ Previous ▾   ⇩ Next ▾   Reply   Reply All   Forward   Flag   Print   Edit   Delete   Rewrap   Inbox ▾

From: aripotter@gasp
Date:
To: letters@buddiescolumn
Subject: Computer maniac?

Dear Buddy,

Last year, my parents bought me a new computer. It's really cool. They told me I had to limit the amount of time I spend playing games or chatting on the computer and do at least one physical activity regularly. Well, the problem is I'm just hooked on my computer. I love talking to my friends after school (on the computer, of course!) and before bed, I play a lot of different games. Sometimes, I don't go to sleep until 1:00 a.m. My parents don't know that because they're already in bed.

I walk to school every day (well, ok, it only takes 10 minutes) but that's about it for physical activity. I know I should be more active but there's nothing that interests me more than my computer. Is this really a problem?

Arianne (14)

Glossary

• fired up = very agitated or enthusiastic

• mistake = error

• get someone off your back = get someone to leave you alone

• hooked on = addicted to, unable to stop using

Helpful LANGUAGE

Dear Sebastian,
Thank you for your question.
No, you don't have to …
No, this is not …
But, I think you should …
You could …
You might …
And don't forget, …
I hope you …

End-of-Unit Task

My Activity Plan

Use what you learned to create a realistic activity schedule.

1. Draw an activity calendar for one month.

● Follow these guidelines.

● Look back at *Canada's Physical Activity Guide* for ideas.

● If possible, use computer software to create your activity plan.

● Look at the model below for help.

• Make a schedule of exercise and activities that you would be willing to do.

• Identify the month and the days of the week.

• Make sure your choices are realistic for you. Include some repetition of the same activities throughout the weeks.

• Do not put in too many activities. You probably won't do them all.

• For each activity, give the following details:
  – where you will do it
  – how long you will do it
  – how many times per week you will do it

• Calculate your total exercise time per week.

ARIANNE'S ACTIVITY PLAN FOR MARCH

Monday	Tuesday	Wednesday	Thursday	Friday	Saturday	Sunday
8:00 a.m. walk the dog	5:30 p.m. yoga class	8:00 a.m. walk the dog	5:30 p.m. jogging with Andy	8:00 a.m. walk the dog	Sleeeeep!	10:00 a.m. snowboarding with the gang
8:00 a.m. walk the dog	5:30 p.m. yoga class	8:00 a.m. walk the dog	5:30 p.m. jogging with Andy	8:00 a.m. walk the dog	Sleeeeep!	
8:00 a.m. walk the dog	5:30 p.m. yoga class	8:00 a.m. walk the dog	5:30 p.m. jogging with Andy	8:00 a.m. walk the dog	Sleeeeep!	10:00 a.m. snowboarding with the gang
8:00 a.m. walk the dog	5:30 p.m. yoga class	8:00 a.m. walk the dog	5:30 p.m. jogging with Andy	8:00 a.m. walk the dog	Sleeeeep!	

MY ACTIVITIES

Activity	Where?	How long?	How many times each week?
Yoga	Church hall	1 hour	1 time
Walk the dog	Around the park	30 minutes	3 times
Jogging	At the schoolyard	45 minutes	1 time
Snowboarding	At the ski hill	2 hours	1 time every 2 weeks
Total exercise time per week: 5 hours and 15 minutes (with snowboarding)			

2. Describe your activities.

● Below your calendar, write a brief summary of the activities you chose.

● Look at the model for help.

● Don't forget to use the writing process and resources.

• Write a short paragraph about the activities you plan to do this month. Your paragraph should be about five sentences long.

• Say why you chose these activities.

• Use at least one modal verb.

I am going to take a yoga class. Yoga is good for getting in shape and for relaxing.
I have to walk the dog anyway, so I will do this on Monday, Wednesday and Friday mornings. My brother can do it the other days!
My friend Andy invited me to go jogging with him on Thursday after school. I might not like jogging, but I will try for one month.
On Sunday mornings, my friends and I would like to go snowboarding if it's not too cold.

3. Go public.

● Put your work on display in the classroom.

• Go around and read each other's work.

• Talk about the different ideas in the activity plans.

• Invite the Phys. Ed. teacher or the principal in to look at the calendars.

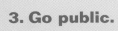
◀◀◀ REWIND

Go through the unit and choose words to add to your vocabulary log.

OUR BLUE PLANET

Canada: A Freshwater Country

Freshwater is very visible in Canada.

Look at the map.

● Name some of the important rivers in Canada.

● Identify the Great Lakes on the map.

● Look at the word box for help.

Word BOX

Churchill
Erie
Fraser
Huron
Mackenzie
Michigan
Ontario
Saint Lawrence
Superior
Yukon
Ottawa
Saguenay

ARCTIC OCEAN

1 YUKON TERRITORIES

3

NORTHWEST TERRITORIES

NUNAVUT

BRITISH COLUMBIA

ALBERTA

4

MANITOBA

PACIFIC OCEAN

2

SASKATCHEWAN

UNITED STATES OF AMERICA

Labrador
Sea

Hudson
Bay

NEWFOUNDLAND & LABRADOR

James
Bay

ONTARIO

QUÉBEC

⑦

PRINCE
EDWARD
ISLAND

NEW
BRUNSWICK

⑥

⑧

⑤

NOVA
SCOTIA

Great

⑩

⑫

Lakes

⑨

⑪

ATLANTIC
OCEAN

0   325 km

The Great Lakes represent the largest surface of freshwater in the world.

● Answer these questions.

What do you know about ...

Canadian rivers?

1. What is the longest river in Canada?
2. Which river is part of the world's greatest river systems and forms the Gulf of Saint Lawrence?
3. What is the longest river in British Colombia?

The Great Lakes?

4. Which one is the largest?
5. Which is the smallest?
6. Niagara Falls is located between two of the Great Lakes. Can you name them?

Your region?

7. What rivers and lakes are there in your region?

● Work with a partner to check your answers.

Bad News

Get the facts on some freshwater issues.

1. Explore the texts.

S T R A T E G Y

Predict.

What clues can you use to predict what the text is about?

A. What water problems do you think each text describes?

a) Canadian wetlands are polluted.

b) People build roads and houses in wetlands.

c) Pollution of their habitat causes mutations in frogs.

d) Frogs are an endangered species.

e) Everyone should use water responsibly.

● Compare answers with a partner. Come to a consensus.

B. Now read the texts carefully.

● Make sure you understand each sentence.

● Use resources to find the meaning of new words.

DISAPPEARING WETLANDS

Wetlands support a variety of wildlife and plants. They also help control flooding because they can hold water just like a sponge. So, they keep the rivers at a normal level in the spring or when there is a heavy rainfall. But every year, more and more of our wetlands disappear. Many are drained to be replaced by housing and roads. Several environmental catastrophes happened before people recognized the importance of these natural areas. Unfortunately, the only thing we can do about it now is to try to save what is left of them.

EVERY DROP COUNTS!

Water is a limited resource – we are still using the same water the dinosaurs used millions of years ago. Using too much water represents a menace to our freshwater supply and everyone should be careful not to overuse water. People who are concerned about this problem can take action. For example, various modern water-saving devices are available. These products can make a big difference in our household water consumption. We can all make the necessary changes to use less water in our lives!

WATER – HOW BAD IS IT?

Some important causes of pollution in our freshwater are chemicals from factories, fertilizers and sewage. Frogs and other amphibians are very sensitive to environmental changes and pollutants. Over the years, many alarming studies show that frogs are mutating. Some are growing extra hind legs or the wrong number of eyes. Are frogs giving us a clue about the overall quality of our water? Fortunately, several laws were created to make sure companies find ecological ways to get rid of their dangerous industrial waste. Also, many farmers are now using fertilizers that are more environmentally friendly.

2. Respond to the texts.

● Organize the information from the texts into a chart.

The problem	Its consequences	Possible solutions

3. Connect with the texts.

● Which one of the three problem areas worries you the most?

● Is one of these problems very present in your community?

Glossary
- devices = inventions
- available = ready
- sensitive = vulnerable
- laws = rules
- supply = reserve

Making a Difference at Home

Small actions can have big results.

1. How much water do you use?

A. Write a list of the ways you use water at home.

● How many litres of water do you think you use every day? Refer to the chart below.

● Compare answers with a classmate.

USE OF WATER AT HOME

This chart shows the percentage of water that we use in our homes.

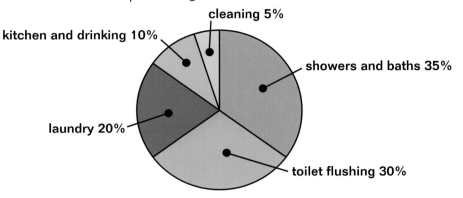

kitchen and drinking 10%

cleaning 5%

showers and baths 35%

laundry 20%

toilet flushing 30%

B. Examine these two charts and answer the questions below.

WATER-USE HABITS

	Typical use	Water-saving habits
Drinking	tap running, 1 litre	Put a water pitcher in the fridge.
Showering	about 19 litres/minute	Wet down, soap up, rinse off.
Taking a bath	150 litres for a full tub	Keep the water at low level.
Flushing the toilet	about 27 litres/flush	Install half-flush device.
Brushing teeth	tap running, 20 litres	Turn water off while brushing.
Washing hands	38 litres	Fill the basin to rinse.
Washing clothes (full cycle)	more than 114 litres	Do only full loads.

2. How can you make a difference?

● Talk about this with a partner: How do you use water responsibly?

● Choose three water-saving habits that seem easy to try.

● Use them in your daily routine!

1. What percentage of water do we use in the kitchen?
2. What percentage of water do we use in the bathroom?
3. What habit uses the most water?
4. Which one uses the least?
5. How many litres of water do we use by flushing the toilet five times a day?
6. If you only had 110 litres of water for a day, how would you use it?

Focus on Form

Prepositions of Place and Movement

1. Show what you know.

Go to pages 96 and 97. Find the prepositions of place and movement in the texts on water-saving gadgets.

2. What prepositions look like

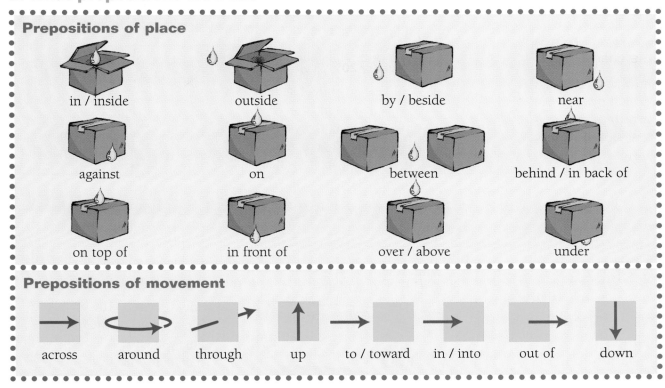

Prepositions of place

in / inside   outside   by / beside   near

against   on   between   behind / in back of

on top of   in front of   over / above   under

Prepositions of movement

across   around   through   up   to / toward   in / into   out of   down

3. Practise.

A. Use prepositions to explain where various objects are placed in the class.

B. Use prepositions to describe what you see in this illustration.

Cool Water-Saving Gadgets

Some cool water-saving devices can help you use less water.

- Read about these six interesting water-saving inventions.

- Form teams.

- Discuss the gadgets with your classmates:
  - Which of these inventions do you find interesting? Why?
  - Which one(s) do you think are not really useful? Why?

Helpful LANGUAGE

Asking for someone's opinion
What do you think?
Do you agree?
Do you think that …?

Giving an opinion
In my opinion …
I think that …

Agreeing with someone
I agree with …
I think you're right.
I think so too.
Exactly!

Disagreeing with someone
I disagree with …
I don't agree with …
I think you're wrong.
I don't think so.

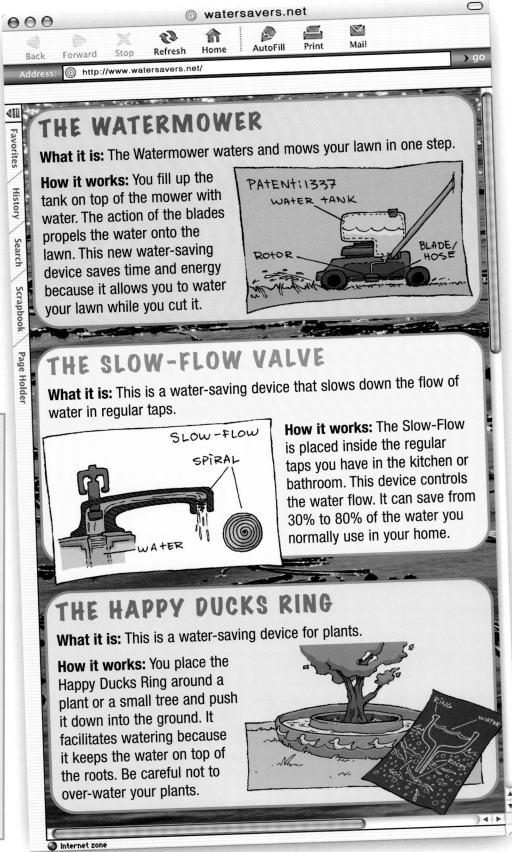

@ watersavers.net

Back Forward Stop Refresh Home AutoFill Print Mail

Address: @ http://www.watersavers.net/) go

THE WATERMOWER

What it is: The Watermower waters and mows your lawn in one step.

How it works: You fill up the tank on top of the mower with water. The action of the blades propels the water onto the lawn. This new water-saving device saves time and energy because it allows you to water your lawn while you cut it.

PATENt:1337
WATER tANK
RotoR
BLADE/HOSE

THE SLOW-FLOW VALVE

What it is: This is a water-saving device that slows down the flow of water in regular taps.

SLOW-FLOW
SPIRAL
WATER

How it works: The Slow-Flow is placed inside the regular taps you have in the kitchen or bathroom. This device controls the water flow. It can save from 30% to 80% of the water you normally use in your home.

THE HAPPY DUCKS RING

What it is: This is a water-saving device for plants.

How it works: You place the Happy Ducks Ring around a plant or a small tree and push it down into the ground. It facilitates watering because it keeps the water on top of the roots. Be careful not to over-water your plants.

RING
WATER
ROOtS

Internet zone

Address: @ http://www.watersavers.net/ › go

Glossary
- mow = to cut grass
- blades = sharp metal for cutting
- propels = pushes out
- allows = permits (verb)
- gadgets = inventions
- spraying = sending fine drops of liquid through the air
- gathering = collecting
- keeps track = monitors

DOG WASH

What it is: This is the ideal gadget to wash your dog and save water. It works the same way as a car wash.

How it works: You place your dog in the Dog Wash tube. The rings inside the tube slowly move, spraying water and soap on the dog. The operation ends with a rinse cycle. You can catch the water in the special reservoir placed under the Dog Wash and use it to wash your car.

RAIN CATCHER

What it is: A great outdoor water-saving accessory that looks like an upside-down umbrella.

How it works: Just walk around with the Rain Catcher as you do with an umbrella. It protects you from the rain while gathering water. The rainwater is collected into the Rain Catcher and goes down a tube that is connected to a small plastic container. You can carry the container in a backpack or on a belt placed around your waist. The rainwater can then be used to wash clothes, water the garden or to wash the car.

WATER SMART WATCH

What it is: This special watch keeps track of your daily water consumption.

How it works: You simply place it around your wrist like a regular watch. A miniature computer keeps count of the number of litres of water you use every time you turn on a water tap or flush the toilet. The mechanism in the watch activates itself at the sound of running water. If you use more than 100 litres of water in a day, the watch will make a beeping sound. Then it will automatically shut off the water in your house for the next hour.

● Look for other water-saving gadgets on the Internet.

Making a Difference in the World

A young boy takes action.

1. Explore the text.

● Look at the photos on this page.

● Read Ryan's story.

● What resources can you use to understand the text?

2. Respond to the text.

● Skim the text to answer the questions.

1. When did Ryan hear about the water problem in Africa?
2. What did Ryan do to earn money?
3. How much does it cost to build a well?
4. Where did Ryan want to build the first well? Why?
5. What did Ryan do after that?

● Compare answers with a partner.

3. Extension

● Do you contribute money or time to environmental projects?

● Find out more about Ryan's Well Foundation and other ecological or environmental projects.

Glossary

• drill = make a hole
• goal = objective
• provide = give

THE POWER OF ONE

When Ryan Hreljac was six years old, he learned from his Grade 1 teacher that people in Africa had to walk many kilometres every day just to get clean water. Ryan was shocked when he heard that children in Africa were sick and sometimes even died because they didn't have access to clean drinking water.

Ryan decided that he wanted to build a well for a village in Africa. He went home and asked his parents for $70 – the amount he thought was necessary to build a well. His parents encouraged him to earn the money by doing extra chores. Ryan vacuumed, washed windows and cleaned the garden. He put all his money into a cookie jar until he saved $70.

Unfortunately, Ryan was in for a bad surprise. He went to give his money to Water Can, a non-profit organization that provides clean water to poor countries. But they told Ryan it actually took $2000 to drill a well rather than $70. Ryan didn't give up! He started to do more chores. News spread of Ryan's goal. People wanted to help and made donations. Four months later, he had enough money. Ryan asked that the well be built near a school in Uganda so that children could have easy access to clean drinking water.

Since then, Ryan's Well Foundation has helped raise over $1.3 million and has supported over 200 water and santitation projects. They provide clean water to people all over Africa and in other developing nations.

End-of-Unit Task

Create a Water-Saving Gadget

Invent a gadget that could help save water.

1. Think of a gadget that can help reduce water usage.

● Work in teams of three or four and brainstorm ideas.

- First choose an area where you feel people use too much water:
  – bathing and personal care
  – laundry
  – cooking and drinking water
  – household cleaning
  – garden and lawn
- Look at pages 96 and 97 for ideas.
- Use the computer or the library to research your topic.
- Decide as a group on the best water-saving idea.

2. Write a first draft.

- Find a name for your invention.
- Explain how your gadget works.

3. Revise your work.

- Go over the checklist to make sure you have everything.
- Correct and adjust your text.

4. Add final touches.

- Do a drawing of your gadget and build a model if you can.

5. Go public.

● Start with a class display of all the water-saving gadgets.

● Look at each other's work.

● Talk about your invention: for example, where you can install it, how it works.

You use this gadget in your bathroom.

The Royal Flush reduces the volume of water in the toilet tank.

Our water-saving invention is called the Royal Flush.

You simply remove the tank lid and place the Royal Flush in the tank of your toilet.

ROYAL FLUSH™

HEADS UP

- In all your team activities, use only English.
- Don't be afraid to make errors. Use your errors to improve.

Go through the unit and choose words to add to your vocabulary log.

◀◀◀ REWIND

Computer Jargon

Computers offer many advantages but they can also cause problems.

A. What are the advantages of using a computer?

● What problems can be caused by computers?

B. The world of computers also has its own particular vocabulary. Match the computer words and expressions with their meanings.

● Compare answers with a partner.

C. Have you experienced any of the problems described on this page?

● Share your experience with a partner.

A cyberspace **B** scam **C** spam

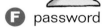

D cyber thief

E hacker

Let's get into this company's data bank.

F password **G** pop-ups **H** virus

What they mean

1. A person who steals your identity or credit card information through the Internet
2. Unwanted e-mail messages that offer or advertise products
3. A program that infects your computer and causes problems
4. An advertisement that appears suddenly when you are using the Internet
5. A word of your own choice that you use to enter programs or sites
6. A person who enters computers in order to steal or corrupt information
7. The universe created by computer systems
8. A fraudulent business offer

Glossary
- fraudulent = false, dishonest

FAST FORWARD ▶▶▶

SuperPals' Adventure in Cyberspace

Time for another SuperPals adventure.

1. Explore the text.

A. What do you remember from the SuperPals story you read in Book A?

S T R A T E G Y

Use what you know.

Are these statements **true** or **false**?

1. The SuperPals got their superpowers during an electric storm.

2. The evil corporation was called Circle.

3. Breaker and Electra go to the same school.

4. Breaker and Electra are twins.

5. Breaker and Electra are just friends.

B. Look over pages 102 to 105.

- What is the story about?

- Where does it take place?

C. These words will help you understand the story.

- Match each word or expression with its definition.

- Add some of these words to your vocabulary log.

Word/Expression	Definition
1. buddy	A. to want to know, to ask yourself
2. evil eye	B. operation to correct vision
3. nasty	C. find a solution
4. an eye for an eye	D. two children born to the same mother at the same time
5. to wonder	E. aggressive, cruel
6. eye surgery	F. stupid
7. solve the mystery	G. friend
8. dumb	H. a trick to catch a person
9. trap	I. an expression meaning revenge
10. twins	J. a malediction, bad magic

2. Follow along.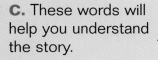

- Read the story as you listen to the recording.

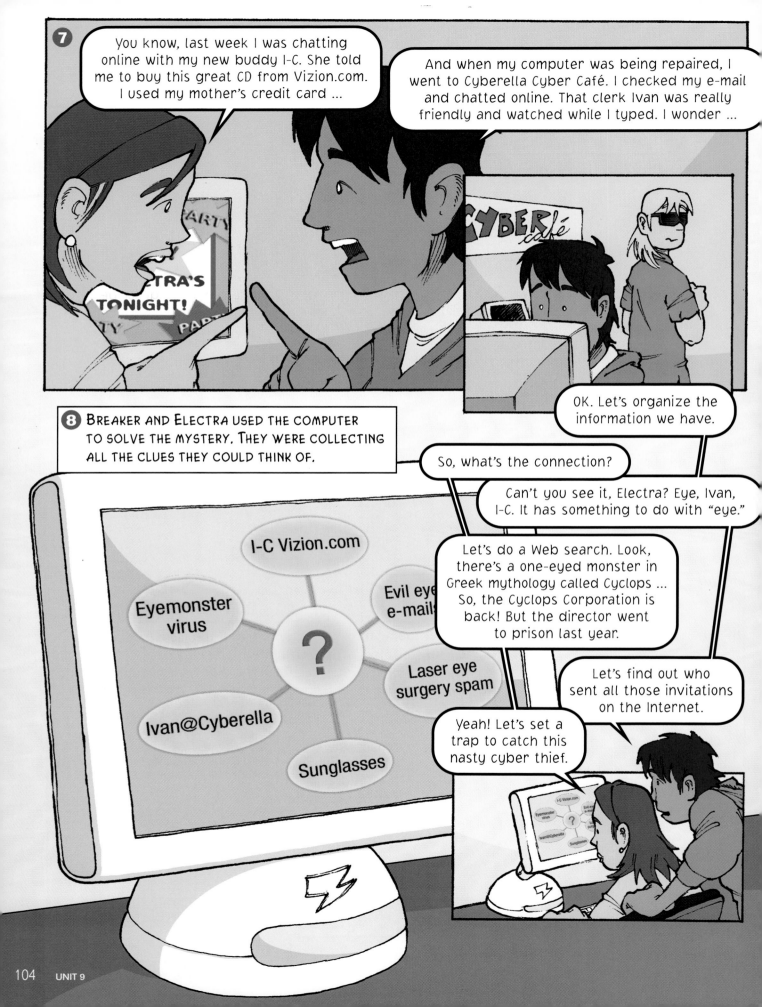

3. Respond to the text.

A. Answer these questions.

B. For you, what was:

● the most interesting part of this story?

● the least interesting part of this story?

1 Why were the SuperPals worried and confused?

2 Where did Breaker go to check his e-mails?

3 Who really sent the evil eye e-mails?

4 Who sent out the invitations to the party at Electra's house?

5 How many party invitations were sent out?

4. Connect with the text.

● Read these Internet safety tips.

● Which ones do you follow?

● Can you suggest other safety tips?

Passwords are secret. Don't share!	Use a cyber-name when you enter a chat room.
Never give out personal information (name, address, telephone number) to a stranger.	Use a credit card only on secure sites. Check the security certificate first.
Don't believe everything you read on the Internet.	Never meet an online friend alone. Go with a parent.
Don't open an e-mail attachment from someone you don't know. They can contain viruses.	Tell your parents or a teacher if someone is sending you mean e-mails or saying things in a chat room that make you uncomfortable.

5. Extension

● Form teams.

● Share experiences about going on the Internet.

● Talk about the advantages and problems of using the Net.

Possible discussion topics:
● e-mailing
● chat rooms
● surfing the Net for information
● shopping online
● downloading music or games
● playing games online

Helpful LANGUAGE

I like e-mailing / chatting / surfing ...
I don't like ...
I thinks it's hard to chat / download / shop / play ...
It's easy to e-mail / shop ...

Comics and Creators

Comic books have existed for over 50 years. Learn about two Canadians who created two very famous superheroes.

1. Work with a partner.

● Together, decide who will read about Todd McFarlane and who will read about Joe Shuster.

● Fill in a profile chart as you read.

• name
• date of birth, place
• personality
• main superhero
• other achievements

● Now ask your partner questions to fill in the second profile chart.

● What do these two creative entrepreneurs have in common?

2. Find out more about comics.

● Survey your classmates. Ask about their favourite comic books.

Helpful LANGUAGE

Do you read comic books?
What's your favourite comic book?
Who's your favourite hero?

Todd McFarlane

Todd McFarlane was born in Calgary, Alberta in 1961, but he spent most of his life in the United States. His first dream was to be a professional baseball player. Todd became fascinated with comic books when he was a teenager. He practised drawing comic book heroes. When a broken ankle ended his baseball career, he decided to become a comic book artist.

In 1984, Todd started working at Marvel comics. He worked very hard on many projects. He showed perseverance and eventually became the main artist of Spider-Man.

Todd needed another challenge. In 1992, he left Marvel Comics and helped to form a new company, Image Comics. He created his own comic book character, Spawn. The first comic book of Spawn sold 1.7 million copies. Then, Todd formed a toy company and made Spawn television cartoons and a Spawn movie.

Joe Shuster

Joe Shuster was born in Toronto in 1914. His family moved to Cleveland when he was 9 years old. He wanted to be a science fiction writer. As a teen, he drew cartoons for his high-school newspaper. Joe first drew a version of Superman in 1931 when he was 17 years old. But it took three years for Joe and his friend Jerry Siegel to develop the superhero. Jerry wrote the stories and Joe did the drawings.

They worked at low-paying jobs, drawing comic strips for Tip Top Comics and Detective Comics. It was hard but they persevered. They had some success with one of their creations, Dr. Occult. In 1938, they finally sold Superman to DC comics. Superman became the most famous hero in comic book history. They produced many comic books. Later, there would be Superman TV shows, cartoons, and movies.

Talking about Past Events

1. Look at the language models.

Who was there?	My best friend Andrea was there.
What happened next?	I called the police.
When did it happen?	It happened at 8:00 on Tuesday evening.
Where were you?	I was at the arena.
Why did you run?	I had no choice.

2. Follow along.

Alex: Hello.

Fiona: Hi, Alex. I have to talk to you. I had a really scary experience.

Alex: When? Where were you?

Fiona: It happened this afternoon at the mall.

Alex: Who was with you?

Fiona: My best friend, Laurie.

Alex: OK. So, what happened?

Fiona: Just outside the jewellery store, we heard someone screaming. Then, we saw an older man falling. He was holding his chest.

Alex: No kidding!

Fiona: His granddaughter was screaming.

Alex: What did you do next?

Fiona: We ran for a security officer. He called 911 right away. The ambulance arrived in five minutes.

Alex: Were you afraid?

Fiona: No, but I was really shaky for a few hours. Well, I have to go.

Alex: OK. See you at school tomorrow.

3. Check it out.

● What questions did Alex use to ask about the event?

● What verbs did Fiona use to describe what happened?

4. Practise.

● With a partner, do a role-play about an event that took place in the past. Choose an event in the box or invent your own.

● Use the telephone conversation as a model. Practise and then share with the class.

Possible events

• a robbery at the electronics store

• a school bus accident

• a lost child at the mall

The Past Continuous

1. Show what you know.

There are two forms of the past tense in the SuperPals story on pages 102 to105: the simple past and the past continuous.

The Cyclops Corporation was doing really well until you ruined everything.

● Look at Iris's speech balloon.

• Which verb is in the simple past? In the past continuous?

• Find three more examples of each form in the story.

2. What the past continuous looks like

The past continuous is made up of two parts:
the simple past of the verb **to be** + the main verb ending in **ing**

Affirmative form

I **was talking** on the phone last night when you called.

You went home because it **was raining**.

They **were eating** lunch in the cafeteria when the alarm went off.

See page 177 in the Reference Section for more on the past continuous.

3. Simple past or past continuous?

These tenses are often used together but they are different.
Observe the difference in the examples below.

• We use the simple past to describe a completed or permanent action in the past.
  They **waited** for the bus for twenty minutes yesterday.

• We use the past continuous to indicate that an action was in progress at a specific moment in the past.
  They **were waiting** for the school bus <u>when the snowstorm started</u>.

4. Practise.

● Complete the sentences, using the past continuous or the simple past tense. See the simple past of irregular verbs on page 176 in the Reference Section.

1. I (play) ❓ a video game when you called.

2. Carlos was sleeping when the telephone (ring) ❓.

3. Vicky (read) ❓ her favourite magazine when I (arrive) ❓.

4. They got out of the pool quickly because a thunderstorm (approach) ❓.

5. I (make) ❓ myself a snack when my mother (come in) ❓.

End-of-Unit Task

A Story Starring ME!

Write a story with you as the main character. It can be something that really happened to you or a dream you had. You can also make up a story.

1. Think about the content of your story.

- Where did it happen?
- Were there other people?
- What happened first? Next?
- How did it end?

2. Write your first draft.

● Look at the models for ideas.

● Use many action words to make your story interesting.

HEADS uP

- Use the past continuous for actions that were in progress. *I was running down the street.*
- Use the simple past for short, completed actions. *Then I saw the police car.*

3. Revise your work.

● Check your verbs, punctuation and spelling.

● Give your story a dramatic title.

AN ADVENTURE IN THE FOREST

GWRAAR!!

One day in June, I was walking in the forest. It was a beautiful, sunny day. The birds were singing. All of a sudden, the sky became black. I heard someone scream. I was running fast. Then ...

I was walking down a very long corridor. Some dogs were barking. I was walking very fast. I saw a light.

Suddenly, I saw the silhouette of a person in front of the light. He was huge. He was walking toward me. I had no choice. I ...

GRRR BARK!!!

BARK!

4. Decide on your final presentation.

● Choose a format.

● Write or record your final version.

On paper, you can
- write your text by hand or use word processing software
- use colour and add photos or illustrations
- write your story in comic strip format

On computer, you can
- do a multi-media presentation
- put the text on screen or you can record it
- add sound effects and music
- use colour and add photos or illustrations

5. Tell your story to your classmates.

● Form groups of four.

● Present your story to your group.

S T R A T E G Y

Encourage yourself and others.

- Be proud of your work.
- Tell others when they do a good job.

H E A D S U P

How to do a presentation to a small group

1. Prepare your presentation. Read over your story.
2. Make a few notes of important parts of your story. (You can't read your story out loud.)
3. Use gestures.
4. Use visual support if possible (illustrations, photos, etc.).
5. Look at your classmates while telling your story.
6. Answer your classmates' questions. To gain time, ask your classmates to repeat the question.

6. Listen to your classmates' stories.

● Decide if they are true or fictional. Try these tips.

- Listen to your classmate tell his or her story.
- To find out if the story is true or fictional, ask for more information and details.

Helpful LANGUAGE

What time was it?
Where did this happen?
Who was with you?
How far did you walk?
So, what happened then?

Go through the unit and choose words to add to your vocabulary log.

◀◀◀ REWIND

ANCIENT GREECE

Looking Back

What do you know about Ancient Greece?

- ● Look at the map.
- • Name some of the Greek islands.
- • Which one is the largest?
- • What seas surrounded Ancient Greece?
- • What were its neighbouring countries?
- • Athens and Sparta were two of the most famous cities of Ancient Greece. Find them on the map.

Glossary

- • neighbouring countries = countries that are next to each other

MACEDONIA

THRACE

EPIRUS

ANCIENT GREECE

PERSIA
EMPIR

Aegean Sea

Ionian Sea

Thebes●
●Delphi

● Athens

Olympia ●

Corinth●

SAMOS

DELOS

NAXOS

Sparta ●

RHODE

Sea of Crete

Mediterranean Sea

CRETE

0   100

CULTURE POP-UP

Ancient Greek civilization existed more than 4000 years ago, but some of its innovations still have an impact on our lives today:

- • democracy
- • trial by jury
- • theatre (tragedy and comedy)
- • mythology
- • the Olympic Games
- • architecture
- • the first alphabet with vowels
- • geometry

- Look at some of the big moments in early Greek history.
  - What do you know about them?

Timeline: Early Greek History

776 BC	The very first Olympic Games are held in Olympia.
About 750 BC	Homer writes the *Odyssey*.
600 BC	The golden age of Greek theatre begins.
507 BC	Democracy is born in Athens.
About 450 BC	Athens takes control of the Greek Empire.
146 BC	Greece is conquered by Rome and becomes part of the Roman Empire.
476 AD	The Roman Empire ends.
1896 AD	The modern Olympic Games begin.
Present Day	

CULTURE POP-UP

BC means "before Christ." It refers to all dates <u>before</u> the birth of Jesus Christ, over 2000 years ago.

AD means "Anno Domini" (in the year of our Lord). It refers to dates <u>after</u> the birth of Christ.

AQUARIUS
AN UNDERWATER CITY

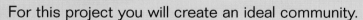

PROJECT: Create a New Community

For this project you will create an ideal community.
- Your community can be a city, small town or village.

Your project must include this information about your community:
- the era it belongs to: past, present or future
- where it is located (continent, country, underwater, in space, on another planet, etc.)
- the social organization of your community
- everyday life: homes, clothing, food, pets
- a special event held in your new community

Plan your project
- Look for ideas as you work through this unit. Use other resources, too.
- Use planning sheets to get organized.
- Do the project in small groups. Have fun!

City States in Ancient Greece

Ancient Greece was divided into small autonomous communities.

● Find the following information in the text.

S T R A T E G Y

Don't forget to use strategies to understand the texts in this unit.

What strategy can you use to find specific information in a text?

1. What a *polis* is
2. The name of two great cities
3. The language that was spoken
4. When boys started military training in Sparta
5. The type of education received by boys in Athens
6. How long boys went to military school in Athens

● Go back to the map on page 112.

- Locate the cities that are mentioned in the text.
- Find the city states that are seaports.

Most Ancient Greeks lived in small city states called *polis*. Many of the city states were seaports. Delphi and Thebes were famous city states, but the greatest ones were Sparta and Athens.

People who lived in the city states all spoke Greek and believed in the same gods. But each city had its own government and customs.

In Sparta, for example, all boys were sent to military school when they were 7 years old. They trained to become soldiers. The other city states mostly counted on Spartans to keep Greece safe.

In Athens, however, boys were educated for both war and peace. They were mainly trained in the arts and went to military school for only two years when they turned 18.

> **PROJECT ALERT**
>
> Communities may have things in common with their neighbours but they also have their individuality. Discuss these points with your teammates:
>
> - What makes your community unique?
> - What subjects are dominant in your schools: arts? languages? sports? science? technology?
>
> Record your ideas on your planning sheets.

Daily Life in Athens

Athens was the largest and the most powerful city state in Ancient Greece. What do we know about the daily life of Athenians?

● Look at the following titles. Find the paragraph that deals with each of them.

- Typical Homes
- A Mediterranean Diet
- Animal Friends
- Simple Fashions

● Write the key information in the chart *All about Athens*.

Glossary

- quarters = rooms
- fabric = cloth

CULTURE POP-UP

Athena was the goddess of wisdom and war. She was also the protective goddess of the city of Athens.

Athenians ate in a very healthy way. They grew olives, grapes and figs, and wheat to make bread. They also kept goats for milk and cheese. Because many city states were near the sea, fish, squid and other seafood were part of their diet.

A typical house was made of stone or clay. The roof and the floor were covered with tiles. Many houses had two or three rooms that were placed around a courtyard. Men and women's quarters were separate. Rich people's homes were nicer and had a kitchen, a room for bathing, a dining room for the men, a special room where women could meet with their friends, slaves' quarters and storerooms.

Men and women had clothing that was quite similar. Both wore tunics called *chitons*. They were long rectangular pieces of cloth

with holes for the head and arms. *Chitons* were made of light fabric. Pins were used to hold them in place at the shoulders. They also wore a belt around the waist. Rich people had fancier *chitons* that were made of expensive cloth and were often decorated to represent the city state in which they lived.

Athenians liked to keep goats, dogs, mice and birds as pets. But cats were not popular animals to have around.

PROJECT ALERT

Discuss these points with your teammates:

- What do the people eat in your ideal community?
- What kind of clothes do they wear?
- What does a typical house look like?
- What kind of pets do people have?

Think of other details you can add to make your community more credible. Record your ideas on your planning sheets.

The Social Structure in Athens

What was it like to be a man, woman or child in Athens in 450 BC?

- Explore the text with a partner.

- Look at each subtitle and at the illustrations. How many categories of people lived in Athens?

- Read each text and find the key words for each of the following:
  - the person's main job or responsibility
  - what the person does for fun
  - what the person cannot do

- Enter the information in the chart *All about Athens*.

Glossary
- overseeing = supervising
- attend = go to, watch
- a minor = a person who is not yet an adult

You are a citizen.

First of all, you are a man. You were born of Athenian parents and received military training. You are probably a businessman, a farmer or in the army. You also spend time overseeing the work of your slaves. You regularly attend public assemblies to discuss and vote on the laws of Athens. For fun, you enjoy wrestling, horseback riding and the famous Olympic Games.

You are the son of a citizen.

You start school when you are about 6 years old and stay until you are 15. You learn music and poetry. At 18, you begin two years of intensive training to become a soldier and a citizen. You cannot vote until you become a citizen.

You are the wife of a citizen.

You are, of course, a woman. Legally, you are considered a minor under the authority of your husband. Your job is to run the household and to have children. If you are rich, your slaves do the housework for you. You cannot attend public assemblies or vote. You can only go to weddings, funerals and some religious festivals. You are not allowed to attend the Olympic Games.

Percentage of population

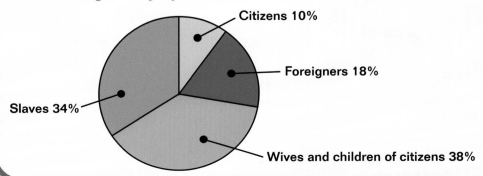

Citizens 10%

Foreigners 18%

Slaves 34%

Wives and children of citizens 38%

You are the daughter of a citizen.

You stay at home until you get married. Your job is to help your mother and, if you are poor, to help out in the fields. Like your mother, you can only go to certain social events. You are not allowed to go to school. Like your mother, you cannot vote or watch the Olympic Games.

You are the slave of a citizen.

You are very important to daily life in Ancient Greece. You clean and cook. You work in the fields, factories, shops, mines, and on ships. You can even be a member of the police force. Your life is not very different from a poor citizen's life. If you are a man, you can teach the male children of the family. However, you cannot participate in political activities and you cannot become a citizen.

You are a foreigner.

You live in Athens but you come from another city state, so you are not considered a citizen. You are probably a merchant or an artisan. You cannot own land and you must pay taxes. You cannot vote or participate in government.

● With the members of your team, look at the information you have entered on the life of people in the chart *All about Athens*.

● Give your opinion.
• What is fair in Athens? What is unfair?
• Was Athens a just society?

⇨ **PROJECT ALERT**

Discuss these points with your teammates:
• What are the roles and responsibilities of the men, the women and the children in your community?
• Is your community a just society?
Record your ideas on your planning sheets.

Government in Athens

Athens was once ruled by kings and nobles, then by tyrants or dictators. In 508 BC, Cleisthenes, an Athenian statesman, introduced a new form of government: democracy.

● Read the following text and enter key information in the chart *All about Athens*.

● Go back to the chart on page 116. What percentage of the population could vote?

The Assembly

The members of the assembly were not elected. All citizens could take part in the meetings of the assembly if they chose to. Every month, citizens met to discuss and vote on the laws. They could choose their leaders. To vote on some issues, there had to be at least 6000 citizens present at the meeting.

The Council of 500

Its members were citizens chosen by lottery every year. They prepared and wrote down the laws to be voted on at the assembly. Some members also worked on administrative committees that were responsible for specific departments like state finances and military affairs.

The Courts

Every year 6000 citizens were selected by lottery to serve on juries, hear cases and vote on the decisions. Citizens had to be 30 years old to be selected.

Then and Now

● Work with a partner.

● Read these statements.

● Compare democracy in Ancient Athens with democracy in Canada today.

● Draw two overlapping circles.

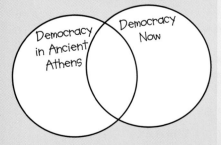

● In the centre, write the similarities. Write the differences on each side.

Statements

1. The government is ruled by the people.
2. Women can vote.
3. All people do not have equal rights.
4. Members are chosen by lottery.
5. People choose their leaders.
6. Only male citizens can become members of the Assembly.
7. The Charter of Rights and Freedoms protects the rights of citizens.
8. Government makes laws that citizens must obey.
9. The representatives meet regularly.
10. There are different levels of government.

PROJECT ALERT

Discuss these points with your teammates. Use the 10 statements above to help you decide.

• What type of government do you want for your community?
• Who makes the rules? Who can vote?
• Is it a democracy or another type of government? Give some details about how it is organized.

Record your ideas on your planning sheets.

Special Events

Athenians believed in the balance of mind and body.
Sports and culture were equally important to them.

- Read about two events that were popular in Ancient Athens.

- Work with a partner and fill in key information in the chart *All about Athens*.

Drama Festivals

These competitions were held annually and lasted several days. Different plays were presented in the daytime in open-air amphitheatres that could accommodate more than 15,000 people. The actors were all men. They wore large masks and elaborate costumes when they performed. The plays were written by poets and authors who were highly respected by the public. Famous Athenian playwrights include Sophocles and Aristophanes.

The Olympic Games

Greeks held many different athletic competitions but the greatest games were the ones held in Olympia. This national festival took place every four years and lasted five consecutive days. Only Greek men were allowed to watch because the athletes competed in the nude. There were nine different events in the competition. The winners were treated as heroes and received a crown of olive leaves.

CULTURE POP-UP

Since 1896, the Olympic Games have only been cancelled three times: in 1916 for World War I, and in 1940 and 1944 for World War II.

PROJECT ALERT

Discuss these points with your teammates.
- What special event is held in your new community?
- When and where does the event take place? Who participates in the event?
- Find a name and draw a logo for your special event.

Glossary
- in the nude = without clothes
- treated as = considered

Working Together

When you work on a project with teammates, you must communicate **in English**.

1. Look at the language models.

● Before you read the conversations, look at the basic steps for doing teamwork.

A. Getting organized

B. Making sure you understand the activity

C. Co-operating during the activity

D. Giving encouragement and praise

● Now look at the language models for each step on page 192 in the Reference Section.

2. Follow along.

● Shawn, Mia, Jeff and Fiona are working on their project. Listen to their conversations.

1

Shawn:	Who wants to read the notes from our project file?
Mia:	I do, but I think we should start by finding a name for our underwater city. What do you think of Aquarium?
Jeff:	I don't really like it. How about Aquarius?
Shawn:	I like it!
Mia:	Me too.
Fiona:	I agree. I think it's a cool name!

2

Shawn:	OK, then. We all agree on Aquarius. Who can read what the first task is?
Fiona:	I can do that. For Task 1, we have to draw a timeline to show the era our city belongs to. And we have to draw a map to show where our city is located.
Jeff:	What do we have in our project file about this?
Mia:	Our city is located under the Pacific Ocean near Hawaii and it's in the future. We decided on the year 4006.
Shawn:	Right! Who can draw a map?
Jeff:	I'll do it on my computer. I can also do the timeline.
Shawn:	Great! Fiona and Mia, let's move on to the second task then.

Shawn: Let's read the instructions for Task 2.

Fiona: OK, we have to talk about the daily life of the people in our city.

Shawn: What did we write on the planning sheets?

Mia: We decided that men and women had similar roles. And that girls and boys went to deep sea diving school. I can write that text.

Shawn: Great. How about making a cardboard model of a typical underwater house?

Fiona: I don't know if we have enough time. I think we can make a floor plan for now.

Mia: I agree. We'll see if we can build a model once we're done with the other tasks.

Jeff: Well, I'm almost done with the map. I can draw the floor plan if you want me to.

Shawn: Don't worry about it. Finish the map and the timeline and I'll draw the house.

Fiona: Good. Listen, I have an idea for clothing. I think it makes it more real if we describe what people wear for their daily activities.

Mia: Let's hear it!

3. Check it out.

● Read the conversations carefully. Find examples of the language they use for each of the basic steps for doing teamwork.

4. Practise.

● Practise the conversations with your teammates.

● As a team, decide who will play Shawn, Mia, Jeff and Fiona.

● Replace the underwater city with your new community. Look over the text to see what information you will need to change.

● Continue the conversation by discussing Tasks 3 and 4 of the project with your teammates.

● Pay attention to good pronunciation. Ask your teacher if you are not sure how to say something.

S T R A T E G Y

Take risks.

Don't be afraid to make errors.

Ask for help.

Your teacher and teammates are there to help you.

PROJECT ALERT

Now it's time to put together all the elements you discussed with your team. Be sure to use team talk.

An Ideal Community

By now you have decided on many aspects of your ideal community. Use your planning sheets to complete the project.

PROJECT: Create a New Community

Pull it all together.

- Divide the work into smaller tasks according to the number of students in your team. Or do all of the tasks together as a team.

Task 1

- Draw a timeline to show the era your community belongs to.

- Draw a map to show where the community is located.

Task 2

- Write a short text about the daily life of the people who live in the community.

- Draw a house or make a model of what a typical house looks like.

- Illustrate how the people are dressed or put together the type of clothing they wear and model the clothes when you do your presentation.

Task 3

- Write a short text to explain how your community is governed.

- Draw a chart to show the levels of government.

Task 4

- Write a short text about a special event your community is famous for.

- As a team, go over the project checklist to make sure you have done everything.

- Comment on each others' work and make any necessary adjustments.

- Make a final version of your part of the project.

- If you can, use a computer. Word processing will make your work easier to read.

Go public.
It's time to share your work with your classmates.

- Go around the class and examine the different communities.

- Decide on the one you like best.

◀◀◀ REWIND

Go through the unit and choose words to add to your vocabulary log.

THE WORK WORLD

Off to Work!

All around us there are people who work. Members of your family work. Just about every adult, young or old, works.

● Some people wake up in the morning and say, "Ugh! I have to go to work again today." Do you know someone like that?

● Others jump out of bed anxious to get to their jobs. Do you know anyone like that?

● Like it or not, work is an essential part of life. So how much do you know about jobs? Work with a partner to answer questions 1 to 10.

What do you call a person who ...

1 takes care of your teeth?

2 designs bridges?

3 cooks in a restaurant?

4 flies an airplane?

5 designs the clothes you wear?

6 puts out fires?

7 programs computers?

8 reports on the news on television or in the newspapers?

9 is the head of a company?

10 takes care of your health?

Skills at Work

What do people actually do at work? Here are some profiles of people in different occupations.

1. Explore the text.

● Look at the job profiles on pages 124–127. Choose the one that interests you the most.

● Complete the reading log.

S T R A T E G Y

Focus your attention.

Look at your reading log. What information should you focus on as you read?

● Use resources to understand the text.

2. Respond to the text.

● Find students who chose the other occupations. Compare the information you found.

Glossary
• gentle = calm, careful
• caring = loving

Job Profile 1: **Veterinarian**

I love seeing animals and their owners happy.

Dr. Jane Anderson is a veterinarian. She works mostly with small animals like dogs and cats. Sometimes, she makes house calls to examine a sick horse.

Regular examinations of pets are a big part of her job. She says it is really important for these animals to have their annual vaccinations, especially if they go outside a lot.

Sometimes, Dr. Anderson performs surgery, mostly in the afternoon hours. She has office hours in the morning. She owns her own business and employs two assistants.

Here is a typical day in Dr. Anderson's work life.

Typical daily activities	Skills that she uses
8:00 a.m. She checks on animals that had surgery the day before and reads test results.	She pays attention to detail. She is gentle and caring.
10:00 a.m. She checks the schedule for the rest of the day and makes any necessary adjustments.	She is organized. She plans and prepares.
10:30 a.m. She examines animals. She discusses possible treatments with their owners.	She is patient, careful and observant. She analyzes the information and communicates with pet owners.
12:30 p.m. She prepares for and does surgery on animals.	She plans and prepares. She identifies problems and finds solutions. She focuses on the procedure.
4:30 p.m. She enters information in the files. She prepares a schedule and assigns tasks to her assistants for the next day.	She decides on priorities. She writes clearly and communicates appropriately.

Job Profile 2: **Flight Attendant**

> You really have to love travelling for this job.

Alec Martinez is a flight attendant. He works for Canada's largest airline.

He has a university degree in Languages and speaks English, French and Spanish fluently. He had seven weeks of training and became familiar with all the procedures on an airplane, including emergencies.

A year ago, he used all his skills when the plane had to make an emergency landing. He was frightened but tried not to show it. Fortunately, most flights are uneventful. Alec is now on a regular three-day schedule. He flies to destinations in Europe once a week.

Here is a typical day in Alec's work life.

Glossary

- uneventful = when nothing unusual happens
- punctual = on time
- get settled = sit down, become comfortable
- sightseeing = visiting tourist attractions and other interesting sites
- headsets = earphones for listening to music or a movie

Typical daily activities	Skills that he uses
6:00 a.m.	
He arrives at the airport and reviews emergency procedures with the crew.	He is responsible and punctual. He pays attention.
7:00 a.m.	
He greets passengers and helps them get settled in the plane.	He is polite and pleasant.
7:30 a.m.	
He explains emergency procedures and checks that everything is ready for take-off.	He communicates appropriately. He focuses on important tasks.
8:00 a.m.	
He hands out newspapers and headsets. He serves drinks and meals during the flight. He takes care of passengers' needs.	He is organized. He works hard physically. He is cheerful and attentive.
3:30 p.m.	
He makes sure the cabin is ready for landing. He helps passengers get off the plane.	He is patient and helpful.
5:30 p.m.	
He goes to a hotel to rest until the next flight. He goes for a walk and does some sightseeing.	He knows how to relax. He is curious about the world.

Job Profile 3: **Meteorologist**

> Everyone blames me when the weather is bad, but I just report on it.

Frank Ryan is a meteorologist. This means that he is a weatherman.

As a boy in Nova Scotia, he saw lots of rainstorms and snowstorms, even a hurricane. He became very interested in weather.

He studied Science at university and then took a one-year program in meteorology.

Now, he reports on the weather for a local TV station. He also writes a column for the newspaper. He works freelance and takes contracts with different employers.

Here is a typical day in Frank's work life.

Glossary
- data = information, statistics

Typical daily activities	Skills that he uses
2:00 p.m. He looks up weather data on various sites. He communicates with the airport weather centre.	He knows how to do research on the computer. He communicates appropriately.
3:00 p.m. He writes his report and prepares the graphics for the six o'clock forecast. He goes over the report and memorizes the details.	He analyzes visual information and data. He uses a computer to write and to prepare graphics. He uses his memory. He practises his presentation.
6:00 p.m. He goes to the TV studio and delivers the weather report.	He reads and speaks well in front of the camera. He concentrates.
7:00 p.m. He takes his dinner break and goes for a walk.	He takes care of himself.
8:00 p.m. He checks the latest weather data for the evening and the next day. He prepares his late-night TV forecast. He writes a weather report for the morning newspapers.	He can do several different jobs at the same time. He can analyze information and write clearly.
10:00 p.m. He delivers the late-night weather report on TV.	He speaks with confidence and energy, even late at night. He stays focused.

Job Profile 4: Personal Trainer and Aerobics Instructor

> To motivate your clients, you have to be in great shape, energetic and enthusiastic.

Diana Lohan is a personal trainer and an aerobics instructor. She took several courses at the local YWCA and has her certification in weight training, cardio training and aerobics, as well as in nutrition, anatomy and CPR.

Because Diana is just starting out as a personal trainer, her job at the fitness centre is just part-time. She hopes that it will become full-time as her client list grows. She supplements her income by teaching an aerobics class in the evening at the YWCA.

Glossary
- CPR: cardiopulmonary resuscitation (to make someone breathe again)

Typical daily activities	Skills that she uses
6:00 a.m.	
She wakes up and eats a good breakfast. She goes to the fitness centre and trains for 90 minutes, then showers.	She practises healthy living and eats nutritious meals. She is disciplined.
9:00 a.m.	
She looks over her client files to review clients' goals and progress and to plan the day's sessions.	She is responsible and organized.
9:30 a.m.	
She trains her first client (weight training, aerobics, etc.). After a half hour break, she trains her second client. Each session lasts 90 minutes.	She is patient and observant. She can assess others and make appropriate training decisions. She encourages others and communicates appropriately.
1:00 p.m.	
She goes home for lunch and a rest.	She takes care of herself.
5:30 p.m.	
She goes to the YWCA and sets up the music for the class.	She is organized and she plans.
6:00 p.m.	
She teaches an aerobics class (Mondays and Wednesday to seniors, Tuesdays and Thursdays to a mixed-age group).	She interacts with people, motivates them and shows leadership. She adapts her aerobics program to the needs of her clientele.

What about Your Interests?

Now let's find out about your interests. They can help you find jobs that are right for you.

1. Read the statements on your activity sheet.

● Follow these instructions.

2. Look at the three circle charts.

● Based on results from the quiz, choose your favourite subject and explore the occupations in that category.

● Choose the occupation that interests you the most.

● Use the Internet to find out more about this job.

Chart 1: THINGS

Things are your thing. You enjoy:

Using tools and machines, making objects with your hands, maintaining or fixing equipment, finding out how things work.

Occupations may be found in:

Engineering, Product Manufacturing, Construction, Repair and Servicing, Transportation, Trades and Technology

The Canada Career Consortium offers this quiz to help you determine what jobs interest you.

- Circle the numbers of the statements that describe you best on your activity sheet.
- Mark an ✘ on the matching numbers in the three boxes in part B on your activity sheet.
- The box with the most numbers marked indicates the area of your strongest interest.

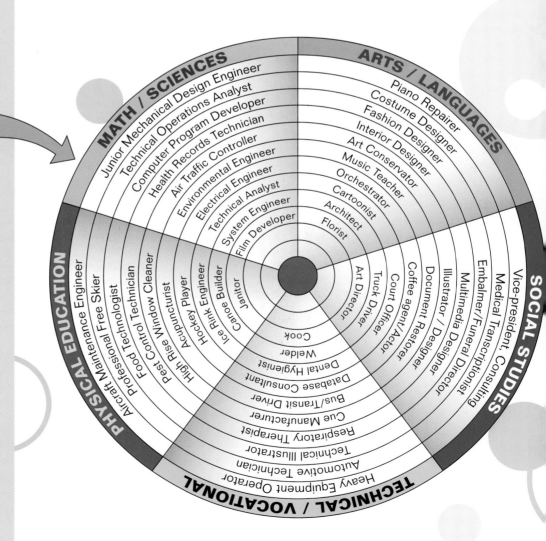

Chart 2: PEOPLE

People are your pastime. You enjoy:

Caring for or helping others, persuading people or negotiating, working as part of a team, leading or supervising others.

Occupations may be found in:

Health Care, Education and Training, Social Work and Counselling, Religion

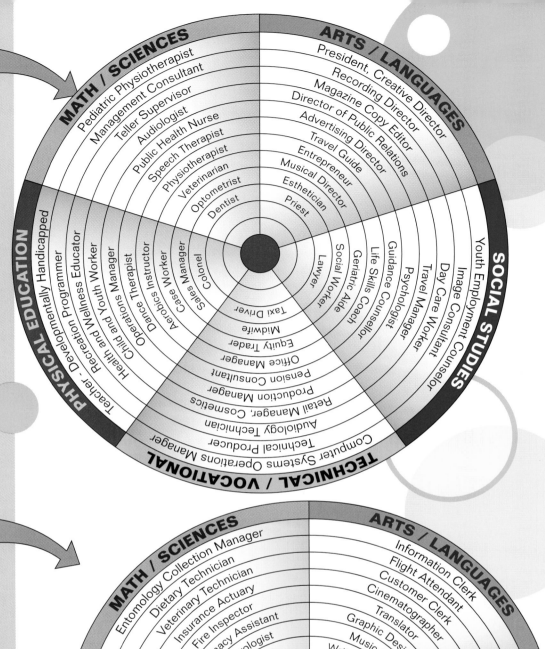

MATH / SCIENCES
- Pediatric Physiotherapist
- Management Consultant
- Teller Supervisor
- Audiologist
- Public Health Nurse
- Speech Therapist
- Physiotherapist
- Veterinarian
- Optometrist
- Dentist

ARTS / LANGUAGES
- President, Creative Director
- Recording Director
- Magazine Copy Editor
- Director of Public Relations
- Advertising Director
- Travel Guide
- Entrepreneur
- Musical Director
- Esthetician
- Priest

PHYSICAL EDUCATION
- Teacher - Developmentally Handicapped
- Development Programmer
- Teacher - Recreation and Wellness Educator
- Health and Youth Worker
- Child and Youth Worker
- Operations Manager
- Dance Instructor
- Aerobics Worker
- Case Manager
- Colonel
- Sales Manager

SOCIAL STUDIES
- Youth Employment Counselor
- Image Consultant
- Day Care Worker
- Travel Manager
- Psychologist
- Guidance Counsellor
- Life Skills Coach
- Geriatric Aide
- Social Worker
- Lawyer

TECHNICAL / VOCATIONAL
- Computer Systems Operations Manager
- Technical Producer
- Audiology Technician
- Retail Manager, Cosmetics
- Production Manager
- Pension Consultant
- Office Manager
- Equity Trader
- Midwife
- Taxi Driver

Chart 3: INFORMATION

You are an information junkie. You enjoy:

Expressing yourself through writing, music, art, doing experiments or researching a topic, solving puzzles or problems, studying or reading.

Occupations may be found in:

Arts and Entertainment, Business and Finance, Scientific Research, Sales and Services, Tourism, Law

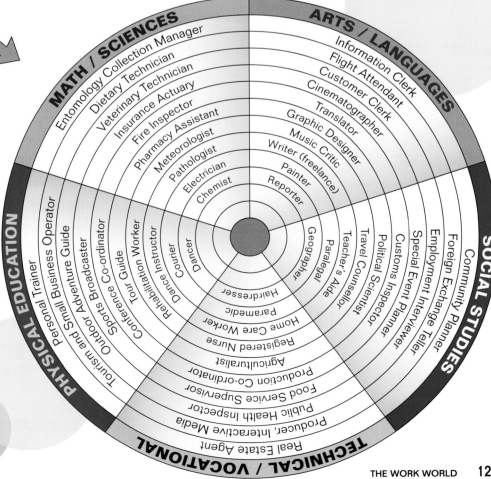

MATH / SCIENCES
- Entomology Collection Manager
- Dietary Technician
- Veterinary Technician
- Insurance Actuary
- Fire Inspector
- Pharmacy Assistant
- Meteorologist
- Pathologist
- Electrician
- Chemist

ARTS / LANGUAGES
- Information Clerk
- Flight Attendant
- Customer Clerk
- Cinematographer
- Translator
- Graphic Designer
- Music Critic
- Writer (freelance)
- Painter
- Reporter

PHYSICAL EDUCATION
- Personal Trainer
- Personal Small Business Operator
- Outdoor Adventure Guide
- Sports Broadcaster
- Tourism Co-ordinator
- Conference Guide
- Tour Worker
- Rehabilitation Instructor
- Courier
- Dance
- Dancer

SOCIAL STUDIES
- Foreign Exchange Planner
- Employment Interviewer
- Special Event Teller
- Customs Planner
- Customs Inspector
- Political Scientist
- Travel Counsellor
- Teacher's Aide
- Paralegal
- Geographer
- Community Planner

TECHNICAL / VOCATIONAL
- Real Estate Agent
- Producer, Interactive Media
- Public Health Inspector
- Food Service Supervisor
- Production Co-ordinator
- Agriculturalist
- Registered Nurse
- Home Care Worker
- Paramedic
- Hairdresser

Life Maps

A life map shows some of the important moments of a person's life. It is a portrait of accomplishments, big or small.

All through our lives, we acquire skills that will help us in our future occupations.

● Read Yolanda's story to see how she evolved. Use your activity sheet to organize the information.

YOLANDA'S STORY

7 But I still love repairing things, so once a week I give workshops for women. I teach them how to repair their own cars.

8 At this point, I am happy with my career choices. But who knows what the future holds for me? I intend to keep an open mind about it.

6 I graduated and went to work for a big computer company.

1 As a child, I loved working with my dad in his garage. Together, we repaired an old sports car. I learned a lot.

2 Later, I figured out how to fix other things around the house, like our toaster and even our fridge!

5 At university, I started in an Education program but didn't like it, so I decided to change to a Computer Sciences program.

3 I loved to teach other kids about mechanical things so I decided to become a teacher.

4 At CEGEP, I took an Arts and Sciences program.

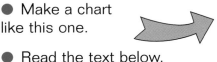

Past, Present and Future

1. Show what you know.

● Make a chart like this one.

● Read the text below. Place the verbs in **bold** in the correct category.

● Indicate if they are in the affirmative (A) or negative (N).

Simple present	Present continuous	Simple past	Past continuous	Future with "will"	Future with "going to"
		was (A)			
		started (A)			

When Adrian **was** just 3 years old, he **started** to play the family piano. He **didn't know** how to read music, so he just **created** his own tunes. Very soon, his mother **noticed** that these tunes **were** quite good. Adrian's parents **consulted** a music specialist who **agreed** to teach him. Today, Adrian **is** 15. At school, he **participates** in sports and **goes** to drama club. He is a good student but he **doesn't like** History or Science very much. He **likes** Math a lot. Outside of school, he **is taking** advanced music classes at a conservatory. Last spring, he **participated** in a music festival and **won** first prize. As he **was performing**, he **realized** that this **was** what he **wanted** to do with the rest of his life. Next summer, he **will go** to Toronto to take special classes at the university. After that, he **is going to take** one year off from school to concentrate on his music.

2. What verb forms look like

This year and last year, you learned about English verb forms in the following tenses:

- simple present
- present continuous
- simple past
- past continuous
- future with *will*
- future with *going to*

You learned how to form these verbs in the following ways:

- affirmative form
- negative form
- question forms (yes/no type questions and information questions)

To review these tenses and forms, see pages 170–179 in the Reference Section.

3. Practise.

● Write a short text about a real or fictional person. Use the text on Adrian as a model.

● Your paragraph should give information about the person in the past, the present and the future. Write at least two sentences for each period. Start with the past.

● Use at least one negative form in your text.

● Show your text to a classmate. Help each other to improve your work.

Discussing Interests and Future Plans

1. Follow along.

● Jenny and Jeff are discussing their interests and what they think they will do in the future.

Jenny: So, what was your favourite pastime when you were 10?

Jeff: Oh, that's easy. I loved playing soccer. What about you?

Jenny: I liked soccer too, but my favourite pastime was Girl Guides.

Jeff: What did you do at Guides?

Jenny: We learned a lot about survival. We went to camps in the winter and the summer. We sang great songs. We just had a lot of fun.
But you could only play soccer in the summer, right?

Jeff: Wrong! We had an indoor program and we played and practised all year.

Jenny: Cool. Do you play soccer now?

Jeff: No, not anymore. I'm playing hockey this year, so there is no time for soccer. What about you? Do you still go to Guides?

Jenny: No, that's over for me, too. But I am part of an orienteering group, once a week.

Jeff: What's orienteering?

Jenny: Well, it's similar to the outdoor survival stuff I did in Guides. We are learning all about moving around in natural habitats without getting lost.

Jeff: Sounds like fun. Are you going to do some kind of outdoor work later?

Jenny: I might. I just love the outdoors. My group is going to visit a class where they teach advanced orienteering. I'm going to check out the career possibilities. And you? Are you going to play sports all your life?

Jeff: Probably, but I doubt that I will make it a career. I'm not really good enough. I'm going to take my time to think about my future and not rush into anything. After all, I'm only 14!

2. Check it out.

● Go through the exchange between Jenny and Jeff. What expressions did they use to ask each other about

- past interests?
- present interests?
- future plans?

● What expressions did Jenny and Jeff use to comment on each other's answers?

3. Try it out.

● Read the conversation with a partner. Decide who will be Jenny and who will be Jeff.

● Pay attention to pronunciation.

● Now, switch roles and read the conversation again.

4. Practise.

● Talk with your partner about your own interests and your future plans:

- Prepare three questions to ask your partner: one about past interests, one about present interests and one about future plans.
- Answer you partner's questions and respond with your own questions. Comment on your partner's statements.

H E A D S U P

Expressions like "What about you?" and "And you?" can be used when asking about the past, present or future. They are very useful to keep a conversation going after you have answered a question.

Glossary
• comment = express an opinion or feelings

S T R A T E G Y

Ask for clarification.

Remember, during a conversation, you can ask for clarification to make sure you understand.

Do you <u>still</u> go to Guides?

Do you mean, <u>now</u>?

Are you going to play sports <u>all your life</u>?

Do you mean, am I going to <u>make a career of sports</u>?

End-of-Unit Task

Life Map to the Year 2020+

Make your personal life map.

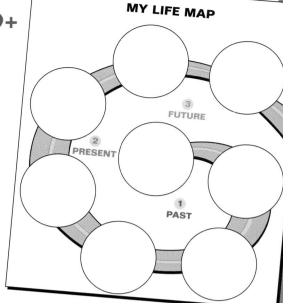

MY LIFE MAP

3 FUTURE

2 PRESENT

1 PAST

1. Follow this plan.

● Make some notes before you start writing.

● Think about
- your past and present interests
- your talents
- the occupations that interest you

- In part 1, show what talents and interests you had when you were 10 or younger.
- In part 2, present some aspects of yourself now.
- In part 3, make predictions for your future.

Helpful LANGUAGE

I am going to …	I think I will …	My life will be …
When I was 8, I could …	I was …	I knew how to …
Today, I like to …	I can…	I participate in …

2. Write your texts.

● Look at the life map on page 130 for examples.

- They must contain examples of verbs in each of the tenses.
- Write at least one sentence in each balloon on your life map. You can write more if you like.

3. Check your work.

- Use the resources in this unit.
- Have a classmate check your work to make sure you have no errors.

4. Illustrate your map.

- You can bring in photos from home to illustrate parts of your life map.
- You can illustrate the different events with drawings or pictures cut out from magazines or taken from the Internet.

5. Go public.

- Post your life map on a bulletin board in the class.
- Go around and read your classmates' life maps. Ask them questions about their experiences and talents.
- Who is predicting the most interesting future in your class?

Go through the unit an choose words to add t your vocabulary log.

◄◄◄ REWIND

UNIT 12 INTER_ACTIVE SUMMER

SUMMER FUN

Another school year is almost finished. What summer activities are you looking forward to?

- How do you feel about these activities?

- Rate each activity using a scale of 0 to 10 points.

Evaluation scale

9–10 Absolutely essential!

7–8 Cool summer fun.

5–6 Ok, if you have no choice.

0–4 Really terrible. I just hope it's a rainy day.

- Write your evaluations in your notebook.

- Share your opinions with a classmate.

Helpful LANGUAGE

My favourite summer activities are …
I gave that activity … points because …
I love … but I hate …
I prefer …
What about you?
Do you really like …?

FAST FORWARD ▶▶▶

1 A pool and pizza party

2 Going to a museum

3 Canoeing or kayaking

4 Cleaning out your closet

5 Playing catch with an old friend

6 Travelling to see relatives

7 Sleeping in a tent

8 A day at the beach with your friends

9 Going to an amusement park

10 Going fishing

Reading Wrap-Up

Use the reading strategies and response process you learned this year to get ready for an active summer.

1. Explore and respond to the text.

● Read about the benefits of regular exercise and summer activities.

● Use the reading log to understand the text. Then, work with a partner to check your answers.

Glossary
- couch potato = a person who watches TV all the time and is inactive
- increase = augment, add to
- decrease = reduce

I feel good about myself!

GET ACTIVE THIS SUMMER!

Don't be a couch potato. Summer is an excellent time to get active.

What's so great about exercise?

Regular exercise will help you feel better in more ways than one. It will increase your strength and fitness, but it also has other benefits. As you exercise, your body produces endorphins. These chemicals are very good. They make you feel happy and relaxed. They will lift your mood when you feel down and may even help you sleep better.

Exercise can also help correct mild depression and low self-esteem. When you increase your strength and energy, you have a better self-image.

And regular exercise will also make you feel that you can reach goals in life. For instance, walking a kilometre was a real challenge at first but now you can walk two kilometres quickly and really enjoy the walk. Being in shape will help you take on new challenges positively.

Will exercise help me look better?

Exercising will make you look better. You will have a healthier and more toned look than people who don't exercise. You will have better posture and flexibility.

Plus, exercising regularly helps you maintain a healthy weight and lose excess body fat. If you eat more calories than you burn, your body stores them away as fat. Exercising helps burn the excess calories stored by your body.

I love being in good shape.

Will regular exercise help me avoid diseases?

Exercising regularly and keeping a healthy weight will decrease your chances of getting diseases such as diabetes, high blood pressure and heart disease.

These diseases used to be rare among teens but they are becoming a problem for teens with very unhealthy lifestyles.

Do I have to exercise a lot?

You don't have to be an Olympic athlete to benefit from exercise. Studies have shown that moderate-intensity activities like walking will provide rewards. Of course, if you wish to develop your cardio-vascular system, high-intensity activities like running are necessary.

Experts suggest that you start slow and gradually increase the length and intensity of your workout. It's always a good idea to get the advice of a physical education teacher or coach.

2. Connect with the text.

● Find a winning formula for yourself. Choose a few summer activities and get active.

3. Go beyond the text.

● Talk about this.

SUMMER ACTIVITIES		
Moderate-intensity activities	High-intensity activities	Other activities that are easy to do
Walking In-line skating Bicycling Swimming Bowling Hip-hop dancing	Running Weight training Basketball Soccer Touch football Martial arts	Frisbee Aerobics in a pool Walking the dog Walking instead of taking the bus Using the stairs instead of the elevator

Helpful
LANGUAGE

I agree.   I disagree.
That is correct.
Yes, that's right.
That is incorrect because …
No, no. That's not right.

Correct or incorrect?

1. To be healthy, you must do high-intensity activities.
2. Teens can develop high blood pressure and diabetes.
3. Touch football is a moderate-intensity activity.
4. Regular exercise makes you feel good.
5. Physical workouts will give you bad posture.

Play *Say It Again, Sam!*

Time to show off your English language skills and have some fun.

1. Find the language resources in this book.

● Where can you review functional language?

● Work with a partner. Practise saying a few expressions from each section.

2. Get ready to play the game.

● Form groups of four.

● Read the instructions and make sure that you understand the game.

3. Play the game.

● Have fun!

HEADS UP

What strategies can you use to help you communicate in English while you play the game?

> Sam sees a spider crawling up Nina's back. He wants to warn her. What does Sam say?

> Sam says, "Watch out, Nina!"

Instructions

● Your group needs a game board, a set of game cards and one die. Each player needs a token.

● Separate the statement cards and the question cards. Place them face down in the spaces on the board.

● Place your tokens on Start.

● To play, you roll the die and move your token to the appropriate square.
  – If your square tells you to pick a card, take the top card.
  – If you land on "Pick any card," choose either a statement card or a question card.
  – Read the instructions on the card aloud to your team.
  – Say your statement or question aloud.
  – The other players decide whether your sentence is complete, correct and appropriate. If necessary, ask the teacher for help.
  – If your sentence is correct, move **forward** the number of squares shown in the circle.
  – If your answer is not correct, move **back** the number of squares shown in the circle.

● The first player to roll the exact number to land on FINISH wins the game.

Start

Say It AGAIN, Sam!

BOARD GAME 4

Pick a statement card
Pick Any card
Pick a question card
Pick Any card
Pick a statement card

Statement
Now, That's Scary!
• Sam sees a spider crawling up Nina's back. He wants to warn her. What does Sam say?

Question
Ancient Greece
• Sam wants to know who will draw the map for the project on Ancient Greece. What does Sam say?

Statement
Our Blue Planet
• Sam wants to give advice to his friend Simon about saving water when he brushes his teeth. What does Sam say?

Question
Shop Smart
• Sam wants your opinion on two music CDs. He can only afford to buy one. What does Sam say?

End-of-Unit Task

Writing Wrap-Up

This year, you used the writing process, vocabulary resources and grammar review to improve your writing. Now, use these tools to write about your dream summer weekend.

1. Plan your weekend.

● Choose activities for the weekend. Look for ideas in the unit and in the Activities box.

● Make a schedule from Friday evening until Sunday evening. Take some notes on possible activities. Fill in activities at various times.

2. Write your first draft.

● Write out your plans. Use the future tenses and modals.

● Need help? Look in the Reference Section.

3. Revise your work.

● Check your verbs, spelling and punctuation.

4. Make your final copy.

5. Share your work with the class.

Activities

- going to a drive-in movie
- riding a horse
- going to a water park
- having a picnic
- staying up late
- going to a big city
- visiting a museum
- playing volleyball
- watching fireworks

MY NOTES

Friday evening:
  19:00 Watching an action movie on DVD with friends
  21:00 Eating pizza with my friends
Saturday morning: Sleeping in until 9:30
  10:00 A huge brunch at my favourite restaurant

A PERFECT SUMMER WEEKEND

On Friday evening, I am going to watch an action movie on DVD with my friends Sacha and Rob. After that we are going to eat an extra large vegetarian pizza. Then we will get some sleep because we are going to have a very busy day tomorrow.
On Saturday morning, I am going to have an excellent brunch and in the afternoon I might ...

◄◄◄ REWIND

ANNEXES

Laura Secord

by Patricia Brock and B.J. Busby

1 One warm summer evening in 1813, there was a loud knock at the door of Laura and James Secord's home in Queenston on the Niagara River. Ever since the Americans declared war on the British a
5 year earlier, Laura was nervous about opening her door. Several months before, invading American troops had attacked the Secord home, stealing or destroying anything of value. Her husband James had also been wounded in battle and still could
10 not walk. The Americans now occupied the town and no-one's home was safe.

There was another **knock**, louder than the first. Laura sent her five children upstairs and went to open the door. Outside stood four American
15 soldiers. They **barged in**, sat at the dining table and demanded food. Laura quickly laid out all the food she had prepared for supper. She then quietly went out the back door. Sitting by an open window, she **overheard** one of the men
20 **boasting** to the others.

"FitzGibbon is finally going to get what he deserves!" he laughed. "In two days, I'll be leading a surprise attack on his headquarters at Beaver Dams and capture every one of his men.
25 The entire Niagara Peninsula will be ours! You will have me, Cyrenius Chaplin, to thank for it."

Laura was **stunned**. She knew that FitzGibbon was the British lieutenant who commanded a nearby outpost. He had recently captured several
30 Americans. But it now appeared that FitzGibbon and his men were in grave danger.

Glossary
- knock = tap on the door
- barged in = came in aggressively
- overheard = heard a private conversation
- boasting = talking confidently
- stunned = shocked

Laura waited in the shadows until the soldiers had left, then ran upstairs to tell her sick husband what she had learned.

35 "Someone has to warn FitzGibbon," said James, "but it can't be me…"

"I'll go!" Laura said. She made preparations to leave the next morning. Just before dawn, Laura departed without a sound. She stopped in St.
40 David's and asked her niece Elizabeth to come with her.

The two women had to stay in the woods to avoid the American guards. This meant a much longer and more difficult journey than the 15 km route along the main road. Soon they were **wading** through **swampland** and baking in the heat. It was too much for Elizabeth. Weak and **exhausted**, she stayed behind with friends while Laura continued alone.

Laura was soon following a **creek** that led to FitzGibbon's outpost. Her **blistered** feet pained her at every step. By nightfall she managed to cross over a fallen tree very close to the outpost, when suddenly she was surrounded by a group of Indians. They were **startled** by her presence and began shouting. Laura was frightened, but she managed to **persuade** the chief to take her to FitzGibbon.

Soon, she was standing barefoot and **bedraggled** before the famous lieutenant. He listened carefully to her story, impressed by her remarkable courage.

"Madam, I believe that we owe you a great deal. Let me begin by offering you food and rest."

Laura was relieved and exhausted. She **fainted** at the lieutenant's feet.

Two days later, when Laura was back safe at home, she learned it was the Americans who were taken by surprise at Beaver Dams. All 462 men surrendered to FitzGibbon.

Glossary
- wading = walking through water
- swampland = wet marsh land
- exhausted = very tired
- creek = small river
- blistered = covered with small, painful bubbles
- startled = surprised
- persuade = convince
- bedraggled = dirty and messy
- fainted = lost consciousness

A Real Christmas

By Josée-Chantal Martineau

1 "It feels like my first Christmas!" thought Frederika, the courageous wife of Baron Von Riedesel. After four years of captivity during the American Revolution, Frederika and her family were free
5 again! Her husband was commander of a German troop. They fought with the British army against the Americans. The General and his family were taken as prisoners. But now, in 1781, they were free once more. They were in Canada now, in the town of
10 Sorel, Québec.

Frederika smiled as she looked out the window of her new house. She watched the delicate, shiny snowflakes fall from the sky. She turned away from that magical scene and went upstairs. Her three
15 older daughters, Augusta, Frederika and Caroline were quietly drawing. Their baby sister, America, was asleep in her small **crib**. Everything looked perfect, but the Baroness felt sadness in the room. "What's wrong, girls?" she asked. The three girls
20 looked **longingly** at their mother and she instantly understood. They were not sad, they were nostalgic. They missed their traditional German Christmas celebrations. Here in Canada, traditions were different. The girls wished they were back in
25 Germany for a true Christmas! Frederika had an idea and **flew out** of the room. For a couple of hours, the girls were left alone. The snow fell harder by the minute.

"Girls! Girls! Come down here! We have a surprise
30 for you!" Frederika and her husband were finally back. They were in the living room holding a beautiful **fir** tree. Their daughters came running down the stairs screaming and laughing with joy. "We are going to have a real Christmas!" shouted
35 Augusta. The house was full of happiness. Everyone began decorating the tree with different ornaments — apples, candies, **gingerbread cakes** and lots of candles. That night was so special. They created the first lighted Christmas tree in Canada!

Glossary

- crib = small bed for a baby
- longingly = showing great desire for something, wanting very much
- flew out = went out rapidly
- fir = an evergreen tree used as a Christmas tree
- gingerbread cakes = molasses cakes flavoured with ginger

Children of the World

By Willie Dunn and Guy Trepanier

1 You were born with a dream
   And with hope in your eyes
   The **elders** have led
   And have bid you to try

5 Child of waters
   Rough with green
   Child of the journey
   Walk with me

   Hold on to your purpose
10 Hang on to your dreams
   Try not to lose direction
   Build your self-esteem

   Child of talent
   Rainbows and trees
15 Palettes of colors
   Of rivers and seas

   Seize the tools
   That will help you win
   Through the culture
20 That you live within

Glossary
- elders = older people
- rough = not smooth

Cherokee Wisdom

First Nations legend

1 An old Cherokee was teaching his grandson about life. "A fight is going on inside me," he said to the boy. "It is a terrible fight, and it is between two wolves."

5 "One is evil — he is anger, envy, regret, greed, arrogance, self pity, guilt, resentment, inferiority, lies, false pride, superiority and ego.

The other is good — he is joy, peace, love, hope, serenity, humility, kindness,
10 benevolence, empathy, generosity, truth, compassion and faith. This same fight is going on inside you, and inside every other person too."

The grandson thought about it for a minute
15 and then asked his grandfather, "Which wolf will win?"

The old Cherokee simply replied, "The one you feed."

The Monkey's Paw

by W.W. Jacobs

I.

1 The night was cold and wet and the wind blew fiercely. Mr. and Mrs. White and their son Herbert sat waiting for their guest.

"There he is," said Herbert, as they heard a loud
5 knock. Mr. White opened the door.

"Hello Morris," said Mr. White happily. "Come in!"

Morris sat on a chair by the fireplace. The two old friends talked about their younger days. Then, Morris began to talk of his travels and mysterious
10 people he had met. He told them the strange tale of the monkey's **paw**.

"Monkey's paw?" said Mrs. White curiously.

"Well, it's just a bit of what you might call magic," said Morris. "Here, look," he said, taking something
15 from his pocket. "It's just an ordinary little paw, dried up like a mummy."

"The legend says that three different men are supposed to have three wishes from it," explained Morris.

20 "Well, did you have three wishes, sir?" asked Herbert, examining the paw.

"I did," Morris said quietly, and his face went white.

"And were your three wishes **granted**?" asked Mrs. White.

25 "They were," responded Morris.

"And has anybody else wished?" inquired the old lady.

"The first man had his three wishes. I don't know what the first two were, but the third was for death.
30 That's how I got the paw." His voice was so grave that the group went silent.

"If you've had your three wishes, then it's no good to you now," said Mr. White. "Why do you keep that old thing?"

35 The soldier shook his head. "I don't know," he said slowly. Then he took the paw and threw it in the fireplace. Mr. White gave a cry of surprise and pulled it out of the fire.

"Don't! You should let it burn!" said Morris.

40 Mr. White examined the bizarre object closely. "How do you make it work?"

"Hold it up in your right hand and make your wish." Then Morris added gravely, "I warn you! Beware of the consequences."

45 "I think you should wish for extra hands for me. I could use the help," said Mrs. White as she got up to prepare the supper.

Glossary
- paw = animal's foot
- granted = given

Her husband looked at the **talisman** and started to laugh. But Morris grabbed Mr. White by the
50 arm. "If you must wish," he said, "wish for something reasonable." Mr. White placed the paw into his pocket.

Later that evening, the family started talking about their guest and the monkey's paw.

55 "Come on father, make a wish," said Herbert, laughing. Mr. White took the paw from his pocket. "I don't know what to wish for," he said slowly. "I have everything I need."

"Why don't you wish for twenty thousand dollars?"
60 Herbert suggested. "Then you can make the final payment on the house."

"Good idea," said Mr. White, with a smile. Holding up the talisman, he wished for twenty thousand dollars. Then he dropped the monkey's paw.

65 "It moved!" he cried with a look of horror. "It **twisted** in my hands like a snake."

"It must have been your imagination," said his wife.

"And I don't see any money," said Herbert as he picked up the object and placed it on the table.

70 Mr. White looked at the paw nervously. "I don't know," he said. "I tell you, it moved."

"I bet you'll find the money on your bed," said Herbert, in a **spooky** voice, "and a horrible monster sitting on top of the dresser — waiting to catch you!"

75 They all laughed and went up to bed.

II.

The next morning the family sat around the breakfast table talking.

"And to think that we almost believed your old friend," said Mrs. White. "And even if such a thing
80 were possible, how could wishing for twenty thousand dollars hurt you?"

"It might fall on your head from the sky," Herbert laughed.

"Morris told me that the things happened so
85 naturally," said Mr. White, "that you might say it was coincidence."

"Well, don't spend the money before I come back from work!" Herbert was still laughing as he left.

His mother laughed also and shook her head.
90 Mr. White didn't seem so sure that it was all a joke.

Later that day, Mrs. White saw a man outside their window. She opened the door and invited the stranger into the house. He seemed nervous.

95 "Mr. And Mrs. White, I'm afraid I have some bad news."

Glossary
- talisman = a magic object
- twisted = turned sideways
- spooky = scary

The old lady jumped. "What is the matter?" she asked quickly. "Has anything happened to Herbert?"

"I'm sorry —" began the visitor.

100 "Is he hurt?" demanded the mother. The visitor nodded.

"Yes, badly hurt," he said quietly, "but he is not in any pain."

"Oh, thank goodness!" said the old woman, 105 "Thank — "

She stopped suddenly as she understood the meaning of his words.

"He was caught in the machinery," said the visitor in a low voice.

110 Mr. White took his wife's hand and held it hard.

The man coughed. "The Company offers their sincere sympathy for your loss," he said. "Because your son worked so hard, the company wishes to offer you compensation."

115 Mr. White dropped his wife's hand. With a look of horror on his face, he asked, "How much?"

"Twenty thousand dollars."

III.

After the funeral, the Whites returned home to an empty, silent house. One night, the old man found 120 himself alone in the bed. The sound of **sobbing** came from the window.

"Come back to bed," he said kindly to his wife. "You will be cold."

"It is colder for my son," said the old woman.

125 Suddenly she cried, "*The paw! The monkey's paw!*"

Mr. White jumped up in alarm. "Where? Where is it? What's the matter?"

"Why didn't I think of it before?" cried Mrs. White happily. "Why didn't *you* think of it?"

130 "Think of what?" he questioned.

Glossary
- sobbing = crying
- snapped = spoke in an angry, quick way

"We still have two wishes," she replied rapidly. "Wish for our boy to be alive again."

"You're crazy!" he said, horrified.

"Get it," she **snapped**, "get it quickly, and wish — 135 Oh, my boy, my boy!"

"Go back to bed," he said. "You don't know what you are saying."

"We had the first wish granted," said Mrs. White. "Why not the second?"

140 "A coincidence," whispered the old man.

"Go and get it and wish," she cried, shaking with excitement.

The old man's voice trembled. "Our son has been dead 10 days. I could only recognize him by his 145 clothing. He was too terrible to look at, how do you think he is now?"

"Do you think I am afraid of my own child?" cried the old woman.

Mr. White went to get the talisman. Fear seized 150 him. What if the wish brought back his son and he was still horribly mutilated?

His wife's face seemed changed when he returned to their room. It looked unnatural. He was afraid of her.

155 "Wish!" she cried, in a strong voice.

"This is evil and crazy," he trembled.

"Wish!" repeated his wife.

He raised his hand. "I wish my son were alive again."

160 The talisman fell to the floor and he looked at it in fear. Then he sat on a chair and waited. After a few minutes, the old man sighed with relief at the failure of the talisman. He went back to bed, and a minute or two afterward, the old woman 165 joined him.

They both lay silently, listening to the ticking of the clock. A stair creaked, and a mouse ran noisily across the ceiling. Suddenly, the couple heard a quiet knock on the front door.

170 They didn't move. The knock was repeated, but still neither of them moved. Then came a third knock.

"What's that?" cried the old woman.

"A rat," said the old man, in shaking tones. "A rat. I'm sure."

175 His wife sat up in bed listening. A loud knock resounded through the house.

"It's Herbert!" she screamed. "It's Herbert!"

She ran to the stairs, but her husband caught her by the arm and held her tightly.

180 "It's my boy. It's Herbert!" she cried. "Why are you holding me? I must open the door!"

"No! Don't let it in," cried the old man.

There was another knock. The old woman ran downstairs. But her husband was on his hands and 185 knees searching wildly on the floor for the monkey's paw. He heard the click of the lock as his wife turned it. And just as she was about to open the door, he found the monkey's paw and frantically made his third and final wish.

190 The knocking stopped suddenly. He heard the door open. A cold wind blew into the house. His wife gave a long cry of disappointment and misery. He rushed down to her side. They looked out at a quiet and deserted road.

E.T.
by Jean Kenward

1 "Extra Terrestrial" they called you, spilling
  suddenly from your chariot of light,
  dark
  in a **darkling** country.
5 Through the **bracken**
  your fingers **fumbled**.
  You were never quite
  with us,
  but only nearly—
10 seemed a stranger,
   yet eager to be friendly,
   not to fight.

   Will it be possible some day to **venture**
   ourselves into your planet?
15 Leave behind
   the guns, the **tanks**, the hatred—
   carry **merely**
   the mild, inquiring **searchlights**
   of the mind?
20 Not wishing to possess
   your place,
   but really
   prove to be simply curious,
   and kind?

Glossary
- darkling = dark, at night
- bracken = small bushes
- fumbled = touched in a clumsy way
- venture = try to go
- tanks = military vehicles
- merely = only
- searchlights = bright lights used to look for something

Save the World for Me
by Maxine Tynes

1 Save the world for me
  save a lake for me to fish in,
  a pond for me to swim in
  a stream to wade in
5 fresh water, clean in wells
  and in drinking glasses.

  Save the world for me
  save the Great Lakes
  and Halifax Harbour
10 save the air to breathe
   over Winnipeg and Vancouver
   over Toronto, Inuvik, Montréal, St. John's
   and everywhere.

   Keep the Bay of Fundy blue
15 and the Arctic tundra white
   keep the Annapolis Valley green
   and my peas and carrots fresh and
   healthy like they're supposed to be
   keep my milk sweet and clean.

20 Save the world for me
   save it from **landfills**
   and from **Chernobyl**
   and from nuclear **weaponry**.

   Save the world for me.

Glossary
- landfills = large areas with garbage buried under the ground
- Chernobyl = site of a nuclear power plant disaster in Ukraine
- weaponry = weapons

For Every Thing There Is a Season

An excerpt from the Bible, Ecclesiastes 3:1-8

1 For every thing there is a season, and a time for every purpose under the sky:
A time to be born, and a time to die; a time to plant, and a time to pick what you planted;
A time to kill, and a time to **heal**; a time to break down, and a time to build up;
A time to **weep**, and a time to laugh; a time to **mourn**, and a time to dance;
5 A time to get, and a time to lose; a time to keep, and a time to throw away;
A time to rip, and a time to sew; a time to be silent, and a time to speak;
A time to love, and a time to hate; a time of war, and a time of peace.

Glossary
- heal = become healthy again
- weep = cry
- mourn = feel sadness

Terry Fox

by Alan Born

> "Somewhere the hurting must stop."
> -Terry Fox (1958-1981)

1 Terry Fox was a natural athlete. When he was 18 years old, he was diagnosed with osteogenic sarcoma — a form of bone cancer. As a result, his right leg was amputated six inches above the right knee. During his recovery he decided to run across Canada to raise
5 awareness of the **suffering** caused by cancer. On April 12, 1980, Terry Fox dipped his artificial foot into the Atlantic Ocean as he began his "Marathon of Hope." He ran 42 km a day. Then, on September 1, 1980, Terry's **relentless** pace was **cut short** by the progression of cancer to his lungs.

10 He died on June 28, 1981, one month before his 23rd birthday. Terry's dream of collecting $1 from every Canadian was realized. The Marathon of Hope raised over $24 million for cancer research.

Today, this hero is commemorated
15 through many awards, research grants, and an annual fund-raising run held in 60 countries in his name.

Glossary
- suffering = feeling pain
- relentless = not stopping
- cut short = stopped

Tiny Men Coming for You

by *Josée-Chantal Martineau*

1 A few years ago, at an old house in the country, Mrs. Ursand sat on her front **porch** crying. Upstairs in their bedroom, her husband was very sick. Mrs. Ursand did not want to cry in front of him, so
5 she left Mr. Ursand with his nurse.

Around midnight, Mrs. Ursand heard something strange coming from the dark road near her house. The sound was far away at first, but it **kept coming** closer. She recognized human voices, something
10 like a song. Suddenly, she saw two big lights. It was a car, but there was no sound of an engine! The only thing she heard was the voices of men and they were definitely singing. Mrs. Ursand felt goosebumps on her arms as it got louder.

15 *Dark at night*
No one to see you
Dark at night
No one to save you
Mr. U
20 *Late at night*
Driving to get you
Mr. U
Just for you
Tiny men coming for you
25 *Tiny men coming for you*

A long, black **hearse** approached the house. To Mrs. Ursand's horror, no one was driving the car. As the car entered her **driveway**, she noticed three extremely small men walking and singing on each
30 side of the hearse. The car stopped. The tiny men walked right past Mrs. Ursand and into the house. They stopped singing. Less than a minute later, they came back holding something shiny and pushed it into the car. They left silently.

35 Frightened, Mrs. Ursand watched the car disappear. At the same moment, the nurse ran outside and announced that Mr. U had died.

Glossary
- porch = terrace
- kept coming = continued to approach
- hearse = car used to carry dead people to the cemetery
- driveway = small road leading to a house

From a Whale Watcher's Diary

by Alexandra Morton

18 June

⟨06:00⟩

1 The morning is perfect for spotting whale **blows**. The wind is light and the sky is clear. As we head north I scan the horizon for blows. There are salmon jumping and lots of birds. I don't know if
5 I'll find whales, but I know that a good place to look at this time of year is in the **inlets**. Salmon follow the herring which come into the inlets to **spawn**. Afterwards the salmon slowly head out to sea again and the whales show up to meet them.

⟨07:40⟩

10 My underwater microphone, called a hydrophone, allows me to hear beneath the surface. Above water all may be quiet, but underwater I can hear cod fish **grunting, otters piping**, many unidentified sounds, and the calls of killer whales. The whales can be
15 very loud and heard 26 km away if there are not too many boat engines around. Once I have located whales with the hydrophone, I can turn on my tape recorder and record their sounds.

Glossary

- blows = water coming from the hole on top of the whale's head
- inlets = a narrow "arm" of water that goes inland from the sea
- spawn = when a fish produces eggs to make babies
- grunting = to make a noise like a pig
- otters = playful water mammals who eat fish
- piping = making a high noise, like a flute
- faint = quiet
- pod = group of whales
- fins = part of a fish or mammal that helps them to swim

⟨09:55⟩

Faint whale calls come over the hydrophone.

⟨10:30⟩

20 I see blows spread across the inlet, heading in. It's A1 **pod**, with Granny in the lead. Nicola is the grandmother in this pod and she is generally out ahead. Close behind her is the adult male, Hardy. At this time of year, the melting glaciers turn the
25 inlet waters pale green. This makes the whales look blacker than ever. All the whales seem happy as they fish. Baby Clio is close to her mother, Tsitika. Her older brothers, Strider, Blackney and Pointer, are out in the middle. With just the points of their
30 back **fins** showing, they look like sharks as they zig-zag up the inlet.

⟨14:30⟩

The whales speed up. The wind is stronger and they look spectacular heading into the waves. But what is the rush? I am confused. One minute everyone is
35 fishing and the next they're racing out of here!

⟨15:30⟩

Now I am really confused. Hardy is out front putting on some kind of show. He is moving in a circle, jumping out of the water, waving his pectoral fin, "spy-hopping" (sticking his head up to look
40 around), and making **sputtering** noises on the surface. The rest of the family is in a line behind him, floating quietly. What is going on?

⟨15:45⟩

Another pod of whales is coming towards us. There is a whale in the lead behaving just like Hardy. I
45 have never seen anything like this. Will I see my first whale fight? I have never heard of anyone seeing killer whales fight. I put the hydrophone back in the water, pull my camera out of its case and get ready to record the event.

⟨16:00⟩

50 The lead whale in the other group is the adult male Top Notch. The pod is A5. Top Notch is closely followed by his brother Foster and their mother Eve. I have not seen this pod since last winter. Top Notch and Hardy are **rubbing** along each other and
55 are soon joined by Eve, Nicola, and the young female, Sharky.

The whales are so gentle with each other! I guess this is a spring reunion. Meetings between killer whales that know each other are always affectionate.
60 These two families are close relatives. We know this because the calls they use are so similar.

As sunset approaches, we leave these two families heading into the inlets. They seem to have fallen asleep together and their blows are rising in unison.

Glossary
- sputtering = making noise with the lips
- rubbing = touching

Lynn Johnston: See You in the Funny Papers!

by Angel Beyde

1 When Canadian humorist Lynn Johnston was a little girl, she loved to read comics in the newspaper together with her grandfather. Her favourites were comic strips like "Peanuts." Lynn wanted to be able
5 to draw cartoons and to make people laugh. Her dream came true! When she grew up, Lynn Johnston became the creator, writer and artist behind the comic strip "For Better or For Worse." This comic strip is read by millions of fans. It appears in
10 newspapers in 23 countries and is translated into 8 languages.

Lynn describes herself as a born artist. She came from a family of creative, humorous people. They recognized Lynn's talent. When her father came to
15 **tuck her in** at night, he would say, "See you in the **funny papers**." From the age of four, Lynn explains, "I would see images appear, my imagination came to life, my right hand drew my thoughts on paper. Even to me, the gift was magic." She originally
20 wanted to be an animator when she attended the Vancouver School of Art. Later, when she couldn't find animation work, she became a cartoonist.

MOM? HOW COME SOME KIDS HAVE PROBLEMS WITH THEIR SKIN AN' OTHERS DON'T?

DUNCAN AN' I BOTH HAVE ZITS BUT GERALD AN' EVA, AN' BECKY, AN' WHOLE BUNCHES OF OTHER KIDS LOOK PERFECT! IT'S **NOT** FAIR!!

HONEY, THERE ARE PLENTY OF GOOD ACNE TREATMENTS ON THE MARKET. WHY DON'T WE GO AND... DON'T SAY THAT WORD! I HATE THAT WORD!

WHERE ARE YOU TWO GOING? TO THE PHARMACY TO PICK UP SOME NO NAME PRODUCTS.

FOR BETTER OR FOR WORSE © 2005 Lynn Johnston Productions. Dist. by Universal Press Syndicate. Reprinted with permission. All rights reserved.

Glossary
- tuck in = make someone comfortable in bed
- funny papers = comics in the newspaper
- whole bunches of = many, a lot of

Lynn Johnston's family is the inspiration for her comic strips. Her main characters are Elly and John Patterson, their children — Michael, Elizabeth, April — and their dog, Edgar. Her stories are both serious and funny, and are about the life of a typical family in the **suburbs**.

"For Better or For Worse" can make you laugh and it can also make you cry. Lynn deals honestly with many difficult issues such as death, bullying, abuse in the home and other family problems. There is also a lot of humour, based on everyday incidents with children, adults and pets. Lynn says, "I have always had a **silly streak** in me that … often got me into trouble. 'For Better or For Worse' lets me put it to good use!"

Lynn Johnston is happy that so many people enjoy her work. Even though she knew she wanted to be a cartoonist, she didn't expect that she could **make a living** that way. Lynn has received many prizes for her art. She received the Order of Canada and she won the Best Syndicated Comic Strip. She was also honoured as Cartoonist of the Year by the National Cartoonist Society in the United States.

Glossary
- suburbs = area just outside the city
- silly streak = sense of fun and humour
- make a living = earn money

FOR BETTER OR FOR WORSE © 2005 Lynn Johnston Productions. Dist. by Universal Press Syndicate. Reprinted with permission. All rights reserved.

What Works Best for Me

An Open Letter from Richardo Keens-Douglas

1 Dear Young Readers and Writers,

My name is Richardo Keens-Douglas and I am a writer. I was born in Grenada. That's an island in the Caribbean Sea. Ever since I was young, I've
5 loved to listen to a good story.

Now I love to write stories too — magical, adventure, fantasy, comedy, serious or scary ones. Most of the characters in my stories are Black. The reason is that I feel there is a need for strong
10 Black characters in books for all young people.

One day, when I was visiting a school, a little Black girl with a big **hairdo** put her hand up. She said, "Excuse me, sir. Do you know a story about a Black princess?" I felt very sad because at that
15 time I didn't know one. So I said to myself, "I will write a story about a Black princess." And that's how *The Nutmeg Princess* came about. The message in that story is, "If you believe in yourself, all things are possible."

20 Ideas for stories can come to you when you least expect them. You have to remember when you find a good idea, though. So I always carry little blank cards or pieces of paper. When I get a good idea for a story, I **jot** it down so I don't forget it.

25 Writing takes a lot of time and hard work. Each story takes a different length of time to write. For some stories, I need to work in complete silence. Other times, I love to put music on.

I always write in a very particular way. You see,
30 I love to write with rhythms and sounds of words. When I am creating a new story, I say the story out loud bit by bit. That's because I need to hear the way the words sound, and the flow of the sentences. Are they short sentences or long
35 sentences? Do the words make you get quiet or sad? So I walk around the house talking to myself, repeating certain phrases over and over until the story feels right and sounds right. Then I put it down on paper.

40 The first and second drafts of my stories are always handwritten. I never use a computer to start creating a story. I feel rushed with a computer. You know what I mean? I always feel as if the computer is sitting there looking at me with its
45 big square face. It seems to say "Hurry up and write. I can't sit here all day waiting for your ideas." Ohhhh, I hate that! I like to take my time and enjoy the writing process.

Once a draft is down on paper, *then* the story goes
50 into the computer, where I do all my rewrites and editing. By the way, I never throw away my first handwritten drafts. It's always good to save them just in case you become really famous. In the future, the original handwritten story might
55 be worth something — you never know!

When I feel the story has all the ingredients to be a good one, I take it to my editor. We sit down and go through the story to see what works or what doesn't work. We check to see if I am
60 repeating myself, or if my sentences are too long. When all of that is done, and we are happy with the finished story, then it goes to be published. And we can all smile. The story is finished.

Now, as I said before, everybody works differently.
65 No matter how hard you work, though, you must love the story you are working on, with all its ups and downs.

Well, my friends, I've got to run now. I just got another idea for a story.

70

Yours truly,
Richardo Keens-Douglas

Once upon a time ...

Glossary
- hairdo = hair style
- jot = write quickly

Daedalus

by *Richard Scrimger*

1 Long ago in ancient Greece, there lived a great inventor named Daedalus. Because of his fame, King Minos of Crete ordered Daedalus to build a maze for him, called the
5 Labyrinth. It was so complicated, so full of twists and dead ends and unexpected turnings, that no one who went in could get out. Minos used the Labyrinth as a kind of **jail** for the Minotaur, a beast who was
10 terrorizing the countryside.

King Minos was so pleased with the Labyrinth that he decided to keep Daedalus in Crete forever, to create more wonderful inventions for him.

Glossary
• jail = prison

Summer

by *Frank Asch*

1 When it's hot
I take my shoes off
I take my shirt off
I take my pants off
5 I take my underwear off
I take my whole body off
and throw it in the river.

River Expedition

- canoeing

- paddling

- portaging

- resting

- travelling

- waving

- boot leather
- buried treasure
  - chest
  - silver
  - gold
- candles
- devil
- mouth of the river

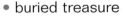

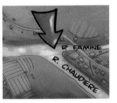

Plus

- Abenakis = First Nation bands now living mainly in Odanak near Sorel and Wolinak near Trois-Rivières
- available = accessible
- current = movement of water in a river
- enjoyed = liked, had a good time
- feast = special meal to celebrate an occasion
- settlement = new community in an undeveloped area
- sickness = illness, malady
- soldiers = members of an army
- town = small city
- view = scenery, panorama

- reached = arrived at
- retreated = abandoned the battle
- shot = (past tense of *to shoot*) injured with a gun

Expressions
- covered bridge = old bridge made of wood with a roof and walls
- early fall = beginning of autumn
- northern tip = north end
- read aloud = read in a normal speaking voice
- started out from = departed from

VOCABULARY

Family Tree

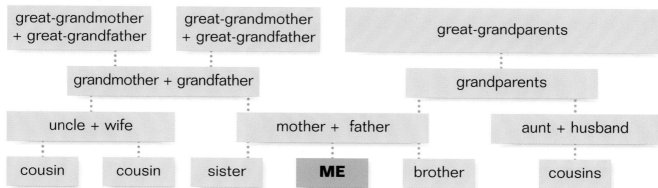

| great-grandmother + great-grandfather | great-grandmother + great-grandfather | great-grandparents |

| grandmother + grandfather | grandparents |

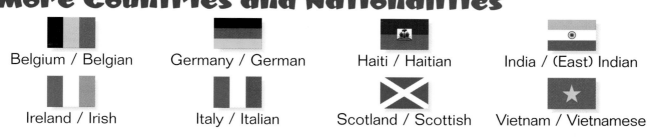

| uncle + wife | mother + father | aunt + husband |

| cousin | cousin | sister | **ME** | brother | cousins |

More Countries and Nationalities

Belgium / Belgian   Germany / German   Haiti / Haitian   India / (East) Indian

Ireland / Irish   Italy / Italian   Scotland / Scottish   Vietnam / Vietnamese

Foods
- brownies = chocolate fudge cake squares
- cabbage rolls = ground meat mixed with rice rolled in a cabbage leaf

- fried plantains = a type of large banana cooked in oil
- griot = fried pork
- shepherd's pie = ground meat covered with mashed potatoes and corn
- seafood = fish, shrimp, lobster, crab and other food from the sea

Plus
- Creole = a language that comes from a combination of French, Spanish, and African-Caribbean cultures
- Gaelic = a language that comes from the Celts
- homeland = country of origin
- legacy = heritage
- roots = social and cultural origins, ancestors
- settlers = immigrants who build new communities in undeveloped areas
- wedding = marriage ceremony
- busy = occupied, no free time
- died = stopped living
- discovering = learning about
- headed = went in the direction of
- immigrated = moved to another country
- traded = exchanged products for money or other products

Expressions
- crossing over = traversing
- mid 1800s = around 1850

VOCABULARY

Signs of Fear

- blushing
- goose bumps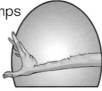
- hiding
- sweating
- screaming
- trembling

Scary Things

- crowds
- cemetery
- dark alley
- horror movie
- needles
- thunder

Plus+

- afraid = terrified, scared
- breaths = respirations
- cautious = careful, taking precautions
- creepy = sinister
- death = end or absence of life
- dizzy = shaky, physically unbalanced
- fear = terror
- owner = proprietor
- phobia = uncontrollable fear
- stranger = unfamiliar person
- scary = frightening
- shy = timid
- thrilling = very exciting

- avoid = stay away from
- bit = past tense of *to bite*
- harm = cause injury, hurt
- hyperventilate = to breathe very fast
- stutter = hesitate when speaking, have difficulty saying certain words
- consciously = intentionally
- unconsciously = unintentionally

Expressions
- face your fear = confront your fear
- flight or fight mode = the instinct to run away from danger or to confront it
- sounds like fun = seems like a good idea
- suffer from = experience

VOCABULARY

Space Travel

- NASA (National Aeronautics and Space Administration)

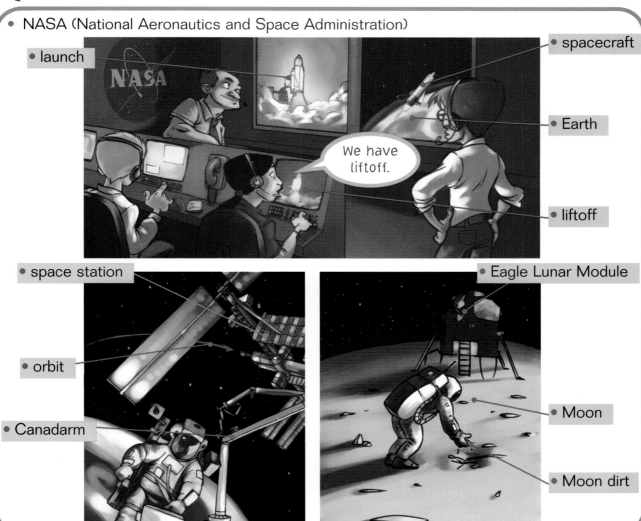

- launch
- spacecraft
- Earth
- We have liftoff.
- liftoff
- space station
- Eagle Lunar Module
- orbit
- Canadarm
- Moon
- Moon dirt

Plus+

- cockpit = part of spacecraft where pilot sits
- crew = the astronauts who work together on a spacecraft
- float = move slowly through the air
- flow = movement
- goal = objective, mission
- race = competition to finish first
- treadmill = exercise machine for walking
- amazing, incredible = wonderful, fantastic
- skyward = up, toward the sky

- aborted = stopped
- flew = simple past of *to fly*
- land = come down from the sky
- tasted = experienced

Expressions
- blasted off = lifted off the ground, departed
- long for = want, wish
- physical fitness = being strong and healthy
- upper bridge = top level of spacecraft

VOCABULARY

Advertising – It's Everywhere

- billboard

- bus shelter poster

- Internet pop-up

- food packaging

- magazine ad

- TV commercial

Get clear, clean-looking skin.

Comparing Prices

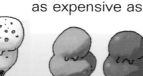

the most expensive — $2.99

more expensive than — $1.99 ... $1.49

as expensive as — $1.49 ... $1.49

less expensive than — $0.99 ... $1.49

the least expensive — $0.75

Plus

- allowance = money your parents give you regularly
- beverages = drinks
- brand = product name
- consumer = person who buys things
- income = the money you make
- receipt = paper that shows how much you paid for something
- slogan = memorable advertising phrase
- catchy = memorable, captivating
- market = advertise an item for sale
- promote = try to make popular, advertise

Expressions

- best deals = best prices
- fine print = special condition usually printed in small type at the bottom of an ad
- impulse spending = spending without planning
- money management = controlling the money you spend
- on sale = at a reduced price
- shop smart = spend money wisely
- tricks of the trade = creative strategies

VOCABULARY

About the Past and the Future

Past	Future

- bonfire = a large outdoor fire to signal a celebration
- cholera = infectious disease resulting in severe gastro-enteritis
- crowds = large groups of people
- Grosse-Île = an island in the middle of the river, east of the city of Québec
- influenza = viral infection or grippe
- lawyer = a person who practises law
- quarantine = a period of isolation for people who may have a disease, from the French word *quarantaine*

- ancestors = members of your family who lived long before you
- consultant = an expert or guide on a specific subject
- get along = be friendly
- interview = ask a series of questions
- immigrants = people who leave a country to live in a new one
- science fiction = stories and movies about the future
- workload = tasks

Plus

Expressions about time
- great time = lots of fun
- hard times = difficult times
- a good time = a good experience
- on time = punctual, at the right time
- time flies = time passes quickly

VOCABULARY

Getting Moving

- wall climbing
- working out
- bending
- hiking
- shovelling snow
- raking leaves
- stretching
- lifting weights
- carrying the groceries

About Weight

- weight (sounds like *wait*) = the amount that you weigh (sounds like *way*)
- weigh = measure how heavy someone is
- gain / put on weight = become heavier
- lose weight = become less heavy
- overweight = too heavy, weighing more than is healthy

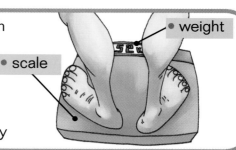

- weight
- scale

Plus

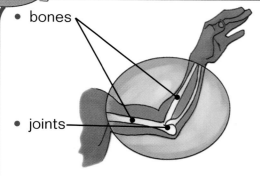

- bones
- joints
- fitness = good physical shape
- health = condition of body and mind

- increase = (do) more
- reduce = (do) less

Expressions
- burn calories = use up energy provided by food
- feel good about yourself = to have strong self-esteem
- good health = being well, without disease
- healthy living = eating, sleeping, exercising the right way

VOCABULARY

The Water Cycle

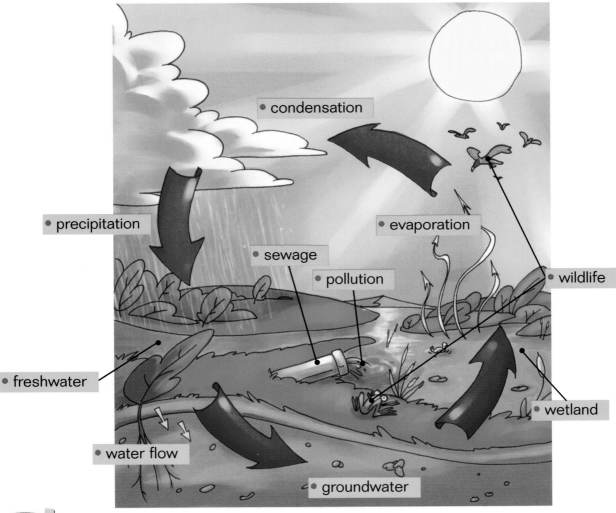

- condensation
- precipitation
- evaporation
- sewage
- pollution
- wildlife
- freshwater
- wetland
- water flow
- groundwater

Plus

- fertilizers = natural or chemical substances used to make the soil more fertile
- flooding = filling a place with water
- flushing = pressing a handle to empty and refill the water in a toilet
- mutation = change
- overall = general
- water pitcher =

- water tap =

Expressions

- endangered species = animals in danger of disappearing
- environmentally friendly = with least impact on the environment
- hind legs = back legs
- industrial wastes = residues that come from industries
- water consumption = the quantity of water we use

Action Words

- sending

- delivering

- receiving

- chatting on-line

<<Skatepro: What's up? Tell me about you.
<< Skihawk: I love to ski all winter. I am fifteen. Do you skate in-line or what?
<<Skatepro: I skate in-line in the summer and I play hockey during the winter.
<<Skihawk: We are really into **COOL** sports. :-)

- knocking down

- screaming

- falling

- hiding

- setting a trap

Plus

- bully = a person who uses his or her physical power to frighten or hurt others
- challenge = something difficult that forces you to make an extra effort
- creator = a person who produces something new
- entrepreneur = a person who takes risks when starting a business
- hedge =

- villain = a bad character in a story or movie

Expressions
- do a Web search = look on the Internet for information
- figure it out = find a solution
- pinned to the ground = held down by force

Daily Life in Athens

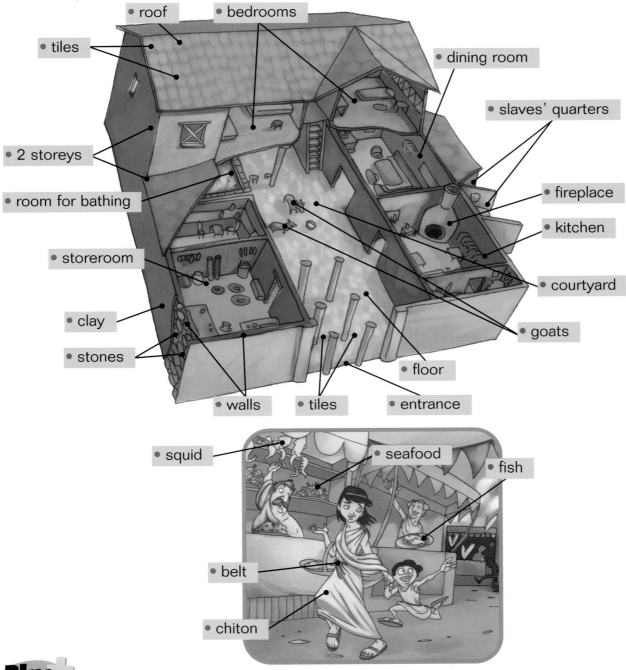

- roof
- bedrooms
- tiles
- dining room
- slaves' quarters
- 2 storeys
- room for bathing
- fireplace
- kitchen
- storeroom
- courtyard
- clay
- goats
- stones
- walls
- tiles
- entrance
- floor
- squid
- seafood
- fish
- belt
- chiton

Plus

- citizen = person who is legally accepted as a member of a city state
- soldier = a member of an army
- social events = social activities people do for enjoyment
- horseback riding =

VOCABULARY

More Jobs

- cinematographer

- customs inspector

- daycare worker

- guidance counsellor

- hairdresser

- heavy equipment operator

- lawyer

- paramedic

- recording director

- real-estate agent

- truck driver

- welder

Plus+

- business = a money-making enterprise
- graphics = pictures shown on TV to show weather patterns
- forecast = weather predictions, report
- skills = capabilities
- staff = personnel
- surgery = operation
- training = specialized education for a job

Expressions

- assign tasks = tell people what jobs to do
- cardio training = exercises that are good for the heart and cardiovascular system

- client files = record of clients' training and fitness goals
- freelance work = work on contract by a self-employed person
- full-time work = working a full week every week
- house call = examination of an animal at its home by the veterinarian
- own your own business = be your own boss
- part-time work = working only part of the day or week
- take pride in = be proud of

Things to Do This Summer

- going to a drive-in movie

- going to a water park

- watching fireworks

- bowling

- playing Frisbee

- hip-hop dancing

- martial arts

- using the stairs

- beach volleyball

Plus+

- benefits, rewards = positive results
- calorie = measure of energy produced by food
- depression = the condition of feeling very sad
- diabetes = a chronic disease resulting in high blood sugar
- endorphins = chemicals produced by your body that make you feel better
- flexibility = ability of the body to bend and move
- mood = the way you feel, attitude
- posture = position of body
- self-esteem = self-respect
- self-image = opinion you have of yourself
- toned = having strength and elasticity

Expressions

- cardiovascular system = heart and blood system
- feel down = feel sad, tired
- lift your mood = make you feel happier

The Simple Present

➡ To be ⬅

Affirmative

Subject	Verb	Rest of sentence
I	am	a good swimmer.

I am / I'm …
You are / You're …
He is / He's …
She is / She's …
It is / It's …
We are / We're …
They are / They're …

Negative

Subject	Verb + not	Rest of sentence
I	am not	a good skater.

I am not / I'm not …
You are not / You're not / You aren't …
He is not / He's not / He isn't …
She is not / She's not / She isn't …
It is not / It's not / It isn't …
We are not / We're not / We aren't …
They are not / They're not / They aren't …

➡ Other verbs ⬅

Affirmative

Subject	Verb	Rest of sentence
I	love	our summer camp.
You	live	in Sept-Îles.
He	asks	for a new bike.
She	needs	new sneakers.
We	own	a motorboat.
They	go	camping often.

Negative

Subject	do+not	Verb	Rest of sentence
I	do not / don't	live	in Sept-Îles.
You	do not / don't	need	new sneakers.
He	does not / doesn't	ask	for a new bike.
She	does not / doesn't	love	summer camp.
We	do not / don't	own	a motorboat.
They	do not / don't go	camping	often.

- Notice the spelling for the third person singular:
  He play**s**.   She goe**s**.   Neville ha**s**.   It bark**s**.

- Notice the verb *to have*:
  I/You/We/They **have**.   BUT   He/She/It **has**.

- Notice the apostrophe. It replaces the missing letter or letters:
  We are ➠ We**'re** (omit the **a**)
  He is not ➠ He **isn't** (omit the **o**)

- Notice the key words that are often used with the simple present tense:
  usually, sometimes, often, always, never, every day / week / month / year / Friday

Questions in the Simple Present

➡ To be ◀

Yes/no questions

Verb	Subject	Rest of question
Am	I	in the right place?
Are	you	interested in yoga?
Is	he	a nice guy?
Is	she	sick today?
Are	we	on the right track?
Are	they	good paddlers?

Information questions

Question word	Verb	Subject	Rest of question
How far	am	I	from the river?
What	are	you	doing?
Why	is	she	there?
Who	is	he?	
Where	are	we?	
How	are	they?	

➡ Other verbs ◀

Yes/no questions

Do/Does	Subject	Verb	Rest of question
Do	I	need	my notes?
Do	you	want	to play soccer?
Does	she	run	every weekend?
Do	we	have	to do part B?
Do	they	like	their new boat?

Information questions

Question word	do/does	Subject	Verb	Rest of question
Where	do	I	go	to register?
What	do	you	want	to do?
Why	does	he	look	so sad?
How	do	we	get	to the pool?
When	do	they	play	basketball?

Notice these question words:

For a person	**Who**	**Who** is that new girl?
For an object or animal	**What**	**What** are you reading?
For a place	**Where**	**Where** do you go swimming?
For a time or date	**When**	**When** is the next train to Drummondville?
For a reason	**Why**	**Why** is he crying?
For a manner	**How**	**How** do you say that in English?
For a quantity	**How** + adjective / adverb	**How many** people live in Matane?
For a possession	**Whose** + noun	**Whose sneakers** are these?
For identification	**Which** + noun	**Which town** is bigger? Granby or Sherbrooke?
For a specific time	**What time**	**What time** is it in Hong Kong?
For a colour	**What colour**	**What colour** is the Italian flag?

The Present Continuous*

Affirmative

With contracted form of *to be*

Subject	Verb to be + ing verb	Rest of the sentence	
I	am paddling	on Lac Mégantic.	I'm paddling …
You	are standing	in the wrong spot.	You're standing …
She	is taking	digital photos of all the sites.	She's taking …
It	is raining.		It's raining.
We	are having	a great time on this excursion.	We're having …
They	are coming	to a turn in the river.	They're coming …

Negative

With contracted form of *to be*

Subject	Verb to be + not + ing verb		Rest of the sentence	
I	am	not looking	at the right web site.	I'm not looking …
You	are	not working	on this project.	You're not working / You aren't …
He	is	not asking	the right questions.	He's not asking / He isn't …
It	is	not snowing.		It's not snowing / It isn't …
We	are	not making	progress.	We're not making / We aren't …
They	are	not talking	to each other.	They're not talking / They aren't …

* The present continuous is also called the present progressive.

Notice these spelling rules:
- **e** is dropped before **ing**:   give-**giving**, take-**taking**, come-**coming**
- final consonant is doubled: sit-**sitting**, run-**running**, travel-**travelling**
- **ie** becomes **y** before **ing**:   lie-**lying**, die-**dying**, tie-**tying**

Use the present continuous to describe:

• **activities that are happening as you speak**
The teacher is coming **right now**.
Other time markers: *at the moment, Look!*

• **actions taking place over a period of time**
He's delivering papers **this summer**.
Other examples: *this afternoon, this week,*
                        this month, this year

• **actions to take place in the near future**
Sophie is taking scuba-diving lessons **next year**.
Other examples: *tonight, at noon, tomorrow, next week, in the evening*

Questions in the Present Continuous

Yes/no questions

Verb	Subject	-ing verb	Rest of sentence
Am	I	travelling	with you?
Are	you	coming	on the trip?
Is	she	leading	the excursion?
Is	he	listening	to the instructions?
Is	it	raining	in the Beauce?
Are	we	leaving	soon?
Are	they	coming	with us?

Short answers

Yes, you **are**.
No, you **are not**. (No, you **aren't**.)
Yes, I **am**.
No, I **am not**. (No, I'm not.)
Yes, she **is**.
No, she **is not** (No, she **isn't**.)
Yes, he **is**.
No, he **is not**. (No, he **isn't**.)
Yes, it **is**.
No, it **is not**. (No, it **isn't**.)
Yes, we **are**.
No, we **are not**. (No, we **aren't**.)
Yes, they **are**.
No, they **are not**. (No, they **aren't**.)

Information questions

Question word	Verb to be	Subject	-ing verb	Rest of question
When	am	I	playing	soccer?
Why	are	you	going	home now?
How	is	he	feeling	this morning?
Where	are	we	eating	lunch?
What	are	they	ordering?	

Who is she speaking to?

The Simple Past

➤ To be ◄

Affirmative			**Negative**		
Subject	*Verb*	*Rest of sentence*	*Subject*	*Verb + not*	*Rest of sentence*
I	**was**	born in Sweden.	I	**was not / wasn't**	a cute baby.
You	**were**	born in Amsterdam.	You	**were not / weren't**	either!
She	**was**	in the garden.	She	**was not / wasn't**	at the wedding.
It	**was**	a busy year.	It	**was not / wasn't**	a good place to live.
We	**were**	born in Lebanon.	We	**were not / weren't**	ready to go.
They	**were**	happy in Gaspé.	They	**were not / weren't**	sure of their roots.

➤ Other verbs ◄

Affirmative of regular verbs			**Negative of regular verbs**		
Subject	*Verb*	*Rest of sentence*	*Subject*	*did not / didn't*	*Verb*
I	**learned**	about my ancestors.	I	**did not / didn't**	learn ...
You	**decided**	to visit your aunt.	You	**did not / didn't**	decide ...
He	**asked**	about his grandfather.	He	**did not / didn't**	ask ...
We	**copied**	all the family trees.	We	**did not / didn't**	copy ...
They	**talked**	a lot about their roots.	They	**did not / didn't**	talk ...

- Form the simple past of regular verbs by adding **ed** to the verb.
  look = look**ed**   play = play**ed**
  If the verb ends in **e**, just add **d**.
  love = lov**ed**   joke = jok**ed**

- Verbs that end in a consonant + **y**, change the **y** to **ied**.
  copy = cop**ied**   study = stud**ied**

- The **ed** ending has three different sounds: **d** as in rained (rain-**d**), **t** as in stopped (stop-**t**) and **id** as in divided (divide-**id**).

- Irregular verbs do not end in **ed**. Their form changes.
  go = **went**   fly = **flew**

- These key words are often used with the simple past tense:
  ago, yesterday, last night / week / month / year / Friday

Affirmative of irregular verbs

Subject	Verb	Rest of sentence
I	found	lots of information.
You	came	from Ontario.
He	thought	his roots were Haitian.
She	wrote	to her cousins in Egypt.
We	bought	a book about genealogy.
They	began	to draw their family trees.

Negative of irregular verbs

Subject	did not / didn't	Verb
I	did not / didn't	find ...
You	did not / didn't	come ...
He	did not / didn't	think ...
She	did not / didn't	write ...
We	did not / didn't	buy ...
They	did not / didn't	begin ...

For a list of common irregular verbs, see page 176.

Questions in the Simple Past

➡ To be ⬅

Yes/no questions

Verb	Subject	Rest of question
Was	I	born in a hospital?
Were	you	born in Canada?
Was	she	funny?
Was	it	hard to leave your country?
Were	we	at the airport on time?
Were	they	happy to immigrate here?

Information questions

Question word	Verb	Subject	Rest of question
Where	was	I	born?
When	were	you	born?
What	was	he	like as a child?
Why	was	it	so important?
Who	were	we	visiting?
How long	were	they	in Europe?

➡ Other verbs ⬅

Yes/no questions

Did	Subject	Verb	Rest of question
Did	I	tell	you about them?
Did	you	know	your grandparents?
Did	he	ask	lots of questions?
Did	it	take	a long time?
Did	we	remember	everything?
Did	they	go	home?

Information questions

Question word	did	Subject	Verb	Rest of question
Where	did	I	grow up?	
What	did	you	eat	for lunch yesterday?
When	did	she	come	to Canada?
Why	did	it	take	so long to get here?
How	did	we	meet?	
Who	did	they	talk	about?

Common Irregular Verbs

Base form	Simple past	Base form	Simple past	Base form	Simple past
babysit	babysat	forget	forgot	see	saw
be (am/is/are)	was/were	forgive	forgave	sell	sold
beat	beat	freeze	froze	send	sent
become	became	get	got	shine	shined/shone
begin	began	give	gave	shoot	shot
bend	bent	go	went	shrink	shrank
bet	bet	grow	grew	shut	shut
bite	bit	hang	hung	sing	sang
bleed	bled	have	had	sink	sank
blow	blew	hear	heard	sit	sat
break	broke	hide	hid	sleep	slept
bring	brought	hit	hit	slide	slid
build	built	hold	held	speak	spoke
burst	burst	hurt	hurt	spend	spent
buy	bought	keep	kept	split	split
catch	caught	kneel	knelt	stand	stood
choose	chose	know	knew	steal	stole
come	came	lay	laid	sting	stung
cost	cost	lead	led	stink	stank
creep	crept	leave	left	strike	struck
cut	cut	lend	lent	sweep	swept
deal	dealt	let	let	swim	swam
dig	dug	lie (down)	lay	take	took
dive	dived/dove	lose	lost	teach	taught
do	did	make	made	tear	tore
draw	drew	mean	meant	tell	told
drink	drank	meet	met	think	thought
drive	drove	pay	paid	throw	threw
eat	ate	put	put	understand	understood
fall	fell	read	read	wake	woke
feed	fed	ride	rode	wear	wore
feel	felt	ring	rang	win	won
fight	fought	run	ran	write	wrote
find	found	say	said		

The Past Continuous*

Affirmative

Subject	Past of to be + verb	Rest of sentence
I	**was reading**	a comic book.
You	**were watching**	TV.
He/She	**was doing**	homework.
It	**was snowing**	outside.
We	**were getting**	impatient.
They	**were hanging out**	at the beach.

Negative

Subject	Past of to be + not + verb	Rest of sentence
I	**was not enjoying**	myself.
You	**weren't cutting**	the grass.
He/She	**was not behaving**	properly.
It	**wasn't going**	very well.
We	**were not talking**	to each other.
They	**weren't asking**	us to be quiet.

* The past continuous is also called the past progressive.

Questions in the Past Continuous

Yes/no questions

Past of to be	Subject	Verb	Rest of question
Was	I	**using**	your pen?
Were	you	**listening**	to that new song?
Was	she	**speaking**	to me?
Was	it	**raining**	when you left?
Were	we	**making**	too much noise?
Were	they	**enjoying**	the amusement park?

Information questions

Question word	Past of to be	Subject	Verb	Rest of question
What	**was**	I	**thinking?**	
Who	**were**	you	**talking**	about?
When	**was**	he	**playing**	guitar?
Where	**was**	it	**going?**	
Why	**were**	we	**doing**	that?
How	**were**	they	**travelling**	to Edmonton?

The Future Tenses
The Future Simple

Affirmative

Subject	will	Verb	Rest of sentence	Contracted form
I	will	go	to CEGEP in Rimouski.	I'll go …
You	will	finish	before me.	You'll finish …
She/He	will	study	in United States, probably.	She/He'll study …
We	will	meet	for high school reunions.	We'll meet …
They	will	work	during summer vacations.	They'll work …

Negative

Subject	will+not	Verb	Rest of sentence	Contracted form
I	will not	take	Science at CEGEP.	I won't take …
You	will not	take	Languages.	You won't take …
It	will not	take	long to get there.	It won't take …
We	will not	find	better friends anywhere.	We won't find …
They	will not	come	home at Christmas.	They won't come …

Question Forms in the Future Simple

Yes/no questions

Will	Subject	Verb	Rest of question
Will	I	have	fun at college?
Will	you	come	to visit me?
Will	he	ask	for more money?
Will	she	become	a teacher?
Will	it	be	fun to work?
Will	we	have	good jobs?
Will	they	hire	us for the summer?

Information questions

Question word	will	Subject	Verb	Rest of question
Where	will	I	be	in 10 years?
How	will	you	spend	your money?
Why	will	he	go	to Japan?
What	will	she	do	now?
When	will	it	end?	
Who	will	we	stay	with?
How long	will	they	study?	

These key words or time markers are used with the future tenses:
- *soon, later, tonight, tomorrow*
- *next Saturday (Sunday, Monday, Tuesday, etc.)*
- *in a minute, in a month, in six months, in one year*
- *on Saturday (Sunday, Monday, Tuesday, etc.)*
- *next week, next month, next year*

The Future with *Going To*

Affirmative

Subject	Verb to be + going to	Rest of sentence
I	am going to	ask them to come over.
You	are going to	get a dog next summer.
She	is going to	watch two movies tonight.
We	are going to	volunteer at the hospital this summer.
They	are going to	camp in the Laurentians.

Contracted form

I'm going to ...
You're going to ...
She's going to ...
We're going to ...
They're going to ...

Negative

Subject	Verb to be + not + going to	Rest of sentence
I	am not going to	travel anywhere this year.
You	are not going to	see your aunt tomorrow.
He	is not going to	see a hockey game downtown.
It	is not going to	be easy to learn Portuguese.
We	are not going to	drive to the Gaspé this summer.
They	are not going to	take the train.

Contracted form

I'm not ...
You're not / you aren't ...
He is not / he isn't ...
It is not / it isn't ...
We are not / we aren't ...
They are not / they aren't ...

Am I going to repair this in time for breakfast?

Question Forms with *Going To*

Yes/no questions

Verb to be	Subject	going to	Rest of question
Am	I	going to	be on time for the concert?
Are	you	going to	play hockey this year?
Is	she	going to	fix the toaster?
Are	we	going to	eat in a restaurant tonight?
Are	they	going to	have a party soon?

Information questions

Question word	Verb to be	Subject	going to	Rest of question
Where	am	I	going to	find the right answers?
What	are	you	going to	do tonight?
When	is	it	going to	start?
Who	are	we	going to	work with on this project?
Which book	are	they	going to	buy?

Modal Auxiliaries

- **Can** indicates an ability or a capacity to do something.
- **May** or **can** indicates permission.
- **Should** indicates a suggestion or giving advice.
- **Must / have to** indicates obligation.
- **Would like to** indicates a wish or desire.
- **Would rather** indicates preference.
- **May / might / could** indicates a possibility OR to answer a question when you are not sure.

Affirmative

I **might** go to my yoga class tonight.
You **can** come with me.
He **should** do more exercise.
She **would** like to join our group.
It **must** be Phys. Ed. day today.
We **have** to practise violin tonight.
They **could** play with us if they are good.

Negative

I **mustn't** forget to stretch, first.
You **cannot / can't** work out all the time.
He **should not / shouldn't** strain his muscles.
She **might not** enjoy that sport.
It **may not** be necessary to wear goggles.
We **would not / wouldn't** want to practise more than twice a week.
They don't **have to** join any team.

How often would you like to walk the dog with me?

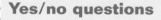

Yes/no questions	Short answers
Can I join your club?	Yes, you **can**. No, you **can't**.
Should you do more exercise?	Yes, I **should**. No, I **shouldn't**.
Could he come to the game with us?	Yes, he **could**. No, he **couldn't**.
Would she rather stay at home?	Yes, she **would**. No, she **wouldn't**.
Could it be the answer?	Yes, it **could**. No, it **couldn't**.
Must we do this now?	Yes, we **must**. No, we **mustn't**.
Do they **have to** wear a helmet?	Yes, they **do**. No, they **don't**.

Information questions

Why do I **have to** take Phys. Ed.?	**When can** he start?
How may I help you?	**Who would like** to draw the map?
Why must we always be late for practice?	**Where should** she buy the equipment?

Comparisons

① Comparisons of equality

- To compare two people or things that are similar or equal, use **as + adjective + as**.
  Andrea is **as tall as** her brother.   My sweater is **as expensive as** my coat.

② Comparisons of superiority or inferiority

To indicate superiority when comparing two people or things, use these forms.

- For short (one-syllable) adjectives, ad **er** + **than** to the adjective.
  cool = My jeans are **cooler than** yours.

- If a short adjective ends with **e**, just add **r**.
  nice = His bike is **nicer than** my bike.

- If a short adjective ends with a vowel and a consonant, double the consonant and add **er**.
  big = **bigger** than   hot = **hotter** than

- If a one-or two-syllable adjective ends with a **y**, change the **y** to **i** and add **er**.
  pretty = **prettier** than

- For longer adjectives (two or more syllables), use **more + adjective + than**.
  exciting = Skateboarding is **more exciting than** jogging.

  To indicate inferiority, use **less + adjective + than**.
  This movie was **less exciting than** the one we saw last week.

> Do not use "less than" with short adjectives (one-syllable). Use an antonym instead.
> Don't say: The red coat is less big than the blue one.
> Say: The red coat is **smaller than** the blue one.

③ Superlative forms

To compare three or more people or things and indicate superiority, use these forms.

- For short (one-syllable) adjectives, use **the + adjective + est**. (If the adjective ends with **e**, just add **st**)
  cool = The red and white sneakers are great. I like the blue and white ones too, but the purple and black ones are **the coolest**.
  smart = A budget is **the smartest** way to manage your money.

- For long adjectives (two or more syllables), use **the most + adjective**.
  beautiful = That is **the most beautiful** dress in the store.
  expensive = I bought **the most expensive** perfume for my aunt.

  To indicate inferiority, use **the least + adjective**.
  This is **the least expensive** gift I bought.

> Some adjectives have irregular comparative and superlative forms.
> good ➡ better than ➡ the best   bad ➡ worse than ➡ the worst
> much / many ➡ more than ➡ the most   far ➡ farther than ➡ the farthest

STRATEGIES AND TOOLS

Interacting Orally

Use these strategies during a conversation.

1 Use what you know.

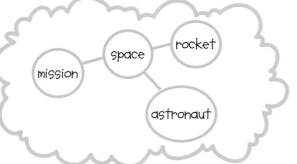

mission — space — rocket
astronaut

2 Focus your attention.

I concentrate. I focus on what's important.

3 Practise.

First I say ... Then, ... I need these words and this question.

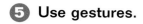

4 It's OK not to understand everything.

I don't understand every word but I get the general idea.

5 Use gestures.

He was very tall.

6 Take your time.

Yes, yes. It's my turn. Just give me a minute.

7 Say it differently.

Hmm. What's that word? He's the leader of the football team. You know the ...

Use these strategies if you have problems.

1 **Ask for help.**

I don't know what to say. I will ask someone to help me.

2 **Be cool.**

Don't panic. Remain calm.

3 **Encourage yourself.**

I know I can do this.

4 **Take chances.**

I think I know this.

5 **Use resources.**

I don't know this. But I know where to find what I need.

Don't forget: functional language is your best resource for conversations.
Use expressions like these:

How do you say … in English?
What's that?
Please repeat that.

• For more functional language, see pages 188–192.
• For vocabulary, see pages 158–169.

STRATEGIES AND TOOLS

Understanding Texts

Use a response process.
You may not need to do every one of these steps. Choose the ones that will help you the most.

① Explore the text.

- Look at the title and illustrations.

- Look for words you know.

- Predict what the text is about.

- Use resources for words you do not know.

- Read each sentence. Stop and ask yourself if you understand it.

- Use other helpful strategies for exploring a text.

To be a better reader, keep a reading log.
- Read a paragraph or a short section.
- Take notes like these.

Strategies

- **Skim.**

This text is about ...

- **Predict.**

I think phobias are ...

- **Make an intelligent guess.**

This must be about ...

- **Take notes.**

What did I just read?
Key words:
Words I need to look up:

Important people:

Important ideas:

Things I need to ask about:

● Scan.

Guillaume **played** an **important role** in **concluding** a peace treaty between the **Iroquois** and the **French**.

❷ Respond to the text.

● What did you discover as you explored the text?

● What was interesting to you?

❸ Connect with the text.

● Do you identify with something or somebody in the text?

● How do you feel about the ideas in the text?

● What is your opinion about the ideas in the text?

● Compare.

I have some of these reactions when I am scared.

❹ Go beyond the text.

● How does it connect with your world?

● Organize information.

Don't forget to use these resources.
• Vocabulary: pages 158–169
• A dictionary

Writing and Producing Texts

The writing process
Use a writing process to improve the quality of your writing.

❶ Preparing to write
- Read the instructions.
- Organize your ideas.
- Take notes.
- Write down some ideas.

❷ Writing a first draft
- Prepare your first draft.
- Refer to the model and instructions.
- Ask for help if you have a problem.

❸ Revising
- Use the checklist.
- Check your writing. Are the ideas clear?
- Ask a classmate to read your text.
- Use grammar and spelling references.
- Make corrections.
- Write the final copy.

❹ Publishing
- Decide on the format of your presentation.
- Present it to the class or your group.

Strategies

- **Plan.**

- **Use what you know.**

- **Ask for help.**

Can you help me? How do you say ...?

- **Check your work.**

- **Be cool. / Don't get nervous.**

OK, stay calm. Don't panic.

Focus your attention.

> now, what's most important?

Take notes.

The production process

❶ Pre-production

- Brainstorm to find a topic.
- Note what you know about the topic.
- Do some research.
- Select the kind of text to produce: poster, computer slide show, Web page.
- Make an outline.

❷ Production

- Create the text.
- Use a writing process.
- Add illustrations, narration, titles.

Co-operate.

❸ Post-production

- Revise the text.
- Add final touches.
- Present the text to the class.

> Don't forget to use these resources.
> - Focus on Form: pages 170–181
> - Vocabulary: pages 158–169

Functional LANGUAGE

Greetings

Hi, there.
Hi, how are you?
How's it going?
How are things?

Fine. / OK, I guess.
Not too bad.
Pretty good. / Could be better.

Identification

What's your name?
Where are you from?
Are you a new student?
Who is she/he?

My name is ...
I'm from ...
Yes I am. / No I'm not.
She's ... / He's ...
This is ...
I'm ...

Leave-Taking

Bye for now.
See you later.
Take care.
See you soon.
Nice to meet you.
Nice talking to you.

Telephone Talk

Calling up
Is ... there?
May I / Can I speak to ..., please?

Answering the phone
Hello?
One moment, please.
Oh, hi ...
Sorry, you have the wrong number.

Starting up a conversation
Hi. What's up?
What's new?
What's happening?

Ending a phone call
Well, I have to go now.
Goodbye.
Bye for now.
See you tomorrow / tonight / next week.

Voice Mail

Typical message on a recorder
Hello, you've reached ...
We're not here now.
Please leave a message.

Leaving a message on a recorder
Hi, it's ... Please call me back at 555-5555.

Fillers and Connectors

What about you?	Ummmmm … / So …
Are you sure?	Well, …
What do you think?	Let me think …
Is this clear?	Just a minute.

Warnings

Be careful!
Watch out!
Pay attention!
Don't …
Stop!

Apologies

I'm sorry.	Excuse me.
I'm really sorry.	I apologize.

Interrupting

Excuse me, but …
Sorry to interrupt.

Permission

May I …?
Can I …?
Is it OK if I …?

Instructions and Classroom Routines

Open your books to page …
Look over the …
Read the …
Take out your notebooks.
Write down …
You have … minutes to do this.
Say it in English.
It's your turn.

Offering Help

Can I help you?
Do you need help?
Can I give you a hand?
Here, let me help you.

Asking for Help

I need help, please.	What does … mean?
Can you help me?	How do we do this?
Help!	How do we write …?
How do you say …?	Is this right?

Functional LANGUAGE

Agreeing

That's right.
I agree because …
I think so, too.
I think you're right.
Exactly!

I agree. / I agree with …
I think … because …

Disagreeing

That's not right.
I disagree. / I don't agree.
I don't think so.
I think you're wrong.
I don't like this choice.

Opinions

What do you think?
I think that …
Do you agree?
In my opinion, …
Do you think that …?

Capabilities

Can you …?
Are you able to …?
What can you do?
What are you good at?

I can … / I can't …

I'm good at …
I'm not good at …

Asking about Feelings, Interests, Tastes, Preferences

In the present
Do you enjoy / like …?
What's his favourite …?
What do you like / prefer?
What would you rather …?
Does she like …?

In the past
What was your favourite … (when you were younger)?
Did you like / enjoy …?
What did you prefer …?
Were you into … ?

Expressing Feelings, Interests, Tastes, Preferences

In the present
I like …
I don't like … / I dislike … / I can't stand …
We prefer …
He loves … He hates …
She'd rather have …
What they like least is …
What they prefer is …
I would choose …
My favourite … is …
My least favourite … is …

In the past
I liked …
I didn't like … / I disliked … / I couldn't stand …
We preferred …
He loved … / He hated …

What they liked least was …
What they preferred was …
My favourite … was …

Asking for Advice

How can I ... ?
What should we ...?
Do you think ...?
Should I ...?
Is this the right thing to do?

Giving Advice

You should ... / You shouldn't ...
Maybe you should ...
I would ...
You could ...
I think you should ...

Decision / Indecision

We decided that ...
My choice is ...
I choose ...

I'm not sure about that.
I don't like that choice.
I can't decide.

Asking for Information

In the present
Yes/no questions
Are you an only child?
Do you have a cat?
Do we both like pasta?

Information questions
What's your favourite dessert?
How many sisters do you have?
When do you play video games?

In the past
Yes/no questions
Did you see anything?
Were you alone?

Information questions
Who was ...?
What happened?
When did it happen?
Where were you?
Why did you ...?

In the future
Yes/no questions
Are you going to ...?
Will she ...?

Information questions
What are you going to ...?
Who's going to ...?
When will you ...?
How will you ...?
Why is he going to ...?
Where will we ... ?

Functional LANGUAGE

Suggestions and Invitations

Let's go … Let's do …
Perhaps we could …
You might try …

Would you like to …?
Why don't you …?
You should …

Do you want to …?
You could …
How about …?

Teamwork and Encouragement

1 Getting organized
Let's do … / Let's go … / Let's try …
How about …?
Would you like to …?
Do you want to be on our team?
Who wants to be … the team leader /
the secretary, etc?
Would you like to do …?
Who wants to do this part?
Who would like to …?
What information do we have already?

**2 Making sure you understand
the activity**
Let's read the instructions first.
What does that word mean?
What are we supposed to do here?
We have to get / do / find …
Let's ask the teacher about this.

3 During the activity
I think this is a good idea.
Do you all agree?   I do. / I don't.
What's your opinion?
Let's try …
No, that doesn't work / make sense.
OK, here's the final decision.
Write that down.

**4 Giving encouragement and
praise**
Good work, everyone!
Cool!
What a good idea! That's a great idea!
We're almost finished. Hang in there.
Good point.
We're doing well.

Discourse Markers

To express a sequence or tell a story, use these transition words.

1	**2**	**3**	**4**
It all began on (day/date).	Soon after, …	And then, …	Finally, …
On (date), …	Next, …	The next thing …	Now …
At (time), …	So, …	Third, …	In the end, …
First, …	Second, …	Fourth, …	Last …
It started when …	After that, …	Then …	Today …
One day, …		After that, …	Since that day, …
		So now …	

PHOTO SOURCES

Pp. 4, 6, 15, 23 (hand), 25, 38, 39, 45 (hand), 53, 65, 74, 77, 86, 108, 120, 121, 132, 133, 188, 189 and 191: The students of Heritage Regional High School were photographed by François Desaulniers. Pp. 4–7: Reduced pages: see photo sources for each page. Pp. 8–14, 17 and 158: The river expedition was photographed by Claude Mathieu (Pub Photo inc.). P. 12: Photo of Québec © Michel Ponomareff / Ponopresse. P. 22: Photos of Marc-Anthony and Virginie courtesy of Gwenn Gauthier. Pp. 23, 26, 29: Photo of Anna courtesy of Pascale Yensen; Big Cheese Photo (boy). Pp. 27, 29: Photo of Sarah courtesy of Klaus Adlhoch. Pp. 28, 31: Photo of Guillaume Couture provided by The Atlas of Canada http://atlas.gc.ca/ © 2006. Produced under licence from Her Majesty the Queen in Right of Canada. Pp. 28, 29: Photo of Tehshang courtesy of Michel Couture. P. 31: Family photos courtesy of Doris Stanutz and Gauthier family. Pp. 32, 33: PhotoDisc (spider, snake). P. 36, 37: PhotoDisc (plant, chicken, horse, spider, bicycle), 7668635 © 2006 Jupiter Images and its representatives (crowd). P. 45: Digital Vision (background photo), 23296047 and 23295687 © 2006 Jupiter Images and its representatives (girl, boy). Pp. 46, 47: Digital Vision (background photo); photos of Laika, Sputnik 2, Apollo 11, Skylab, Mir and International Space Station courtesy of NASA (National Aeronautics and Space Administration). P. 48: Photos of astronauts and Canadarm by permission of the Canadian Space Agency; photo of Neil Armstrong courtesy of NASA; Digital Vision (footprint on the Moon). P. 49: Photo by permission of Julie Payette and the Canadian Space Agency. P. 50: 23295567 © 2006 Jupiter Images and its representatives (boy). P. 52: Digital Vision (astronaut). P. 55: Rubberball (blond girl); Big Cheese Photo (girl on cover). P. 60: 861039 © ShutterStock (TV); 26547934 © 2006 Jupiter Images and its representatives ("New"). P. 62: Rubberball (four teens); 22879512 © 2006 Jupiter Images and its representatives (wallet). P. 63: 19065805 © 2006 Jupiter Images and its representatives (boy); Creativ Collection (piggy bank). P. 64: 23278131 and 23278341 © 2006 Jupiter Images and its representatives (change, penny jar). P. 66: PhotoDisc (keyboard). P. 78: Photo of baby courtesy of Michael O'Neill; 30363540, 23111668 and 9818975 © 2006 Jupiter Images and its representatives (boy, teen and car). P. 80: 227127619 and 23289195 © 2006 Jupiter Images and its representatives (boy, girl). Pp. 81–83: Cover and pages of *Canada's Physical Activity Guide for Youth*, Public Health Agency of Canada © 2002, reproduced with the permission of the Minister of Public Works and Government Services. P. 84: Rubberball (teen). P. 87: 22726935 © 2006 Jupiter Images and its representatives (teen at computer). P. 88: PhotoDisc (laptop). P. 92: Photo of deformed frogs © Joseph Kiesecker. P. 93: 7723703 © 2006 Jupiter Images and its representatives (wetlands). P. 94: 19128401, 19389853, 9970305 and 9979139 © 2006 Jupiter Images and its representatives (bathroom and kitchen sinks, toilet and shower). P. 97: PhotoDisc (mouse). P. 98: Photos by permission of the Ryan's Well Foundation (www.ryanswell.ca). P. 106: 10047200 © 2006 Jupiter Images and its representatives (monitor). P. 107: Photo of Spawn © Corbis Sygma; photo of Superman © OM Misc / Topfoto / Ponopresse. P. 111: 23074720 © 2006 Jupiter Images and its representatives (teen). P. 112: 16468596 © 2006 Jupiter Images and its representatives (Athens). P. 115: 7732046 © 2006 Jupiter Images and its representatives (goddess Athena). P. 122: 22799234 © 2006 Jupiter Images and its representatives (scuba diver); PhotoDisc (keyboard). Pp. 124–127: 23278887, 23560359, 23288655, 28562740 © 2006 Jupiter Images and its representatives (job photos). Pp. 136, 137: 22712739, 23420175 and 23418899 © 2006 Jupiter Images and its representatives (teens); PhotoDisc (soccer ball, football). P. 150: Photo of Terry Fox taken by Boris Spremo, used by permission of the Toronto Star. P. 154: Photo courtesy of Lynn Johnston Productions and Universal Press Syndicate.

TEXT SOURCES

Pp. 32–34: Quiz and body chart inspired by an article in *OWL* Magazine, 2001.
Pp. 36, 37: Text inspired by an article in *OWL* Magazine, 2001.
Pp. 46, 47, 50: Adapted from information published by NASA (National Aeronautics and Space Administration) on its Web site.
P. 49: E-mail (translated and adapted) courtesy of Astronaut Julie Payette and the Canadian Space Agency.
P. 52: Adapted from "How can I become an astronaut?" by permission of the Canadian Space Agency.
Pp. 81–83: Cover and double page reprinted from *Canada's Physical Activity Guide for Youth*, Public Health Agency of Canada © 2002. Reproduced with permission of Minister of Public Works and Government Services Canada, 2006.
P. 94: Information in charts from "Water Use in the Home" from Environment Canada's Freshwater Web site (www.ec.gc.ca/water), Environment Canada, 2005. Reproduced with the permission of the Minister of Public Works and Government Services, 2006.
P. 98: Text inspired by information from the Ryan's Well Web site (http://ryanswell.ca), 2006.
Pp. 124–127: Job profiles adapted from *Destination 2020*, published by the Canada Career Consortium.
Pp. 128, 129: "Your Interests" quiz, circle charts from *Destination 2020*, published by the Canada Career Consortium.

Pp. 130, 134: The life maps concept adapted from *Destination 2020,* published by the Canada Career Consortium.
Pp. 141, 142: "Laura Secord" © Canada Post. Reproduced with permission.
P. 143: "A Real Christmas" © Josée-Chantal Martineau, adapted by permission of the author.
P. 144: "Children of the World" © William Laurence Dunn/Groupe Concept Musique Les Éditions Guy Trépanier (SODRAC).
P. 144: "Cherokee Wisdom" First Nations legend, in public domain, author unknown.
Pp. 145–148: "The Monkey's Paw" by W.W. Jacobs, in public domain.
P. 149: "E.T." © Jean Kenward, reprinted by permission of Jean Kenward.
P. 149: "Save the World for Me" © Maxine Tynes. Maxine Tynes is a poet, author and educator who lives and works in Dartmouth, Nova Scotia.
P. 150: "For Every Thing There Is a Season" adapted from Ecclesiastes 3:1–8, the Bible, King James Version, in public domain.
P. 150: "Terry Fox" adapted from the article by Alan Born © Library and Archives Canada. Reproduced with the permission of the Minister of Public Works and Government Services Canada, 2005.
P. 151: "Tiny Men Coming for You" © Josée-Chantal Martineau, adapted by permission of the author.
Pp. 152–153: "From a Whale Watcher's Diary" © Alexandra Morton, excerpt adapted by permission of the author.
Pp. 154–155: "Lynn Johnston: See You in the Funny Papers!" © Angel Beyde. FOR BETTER OR FOR WORSE comics © 2005 Lynn Johnston Productions. Distributed by Universal Press Syndicate. Reprinted with permission. All rights reserved.
P. 156: "What Works Best for Me" by permission of Toronto-based author/actor/storyteller/playwright Richardo Keens-Douglas.
P. 157: "Daedalus" excerpt from "Wings to the Sun," by permission of Richard Scrimger.
P. 157: "Summer" by permission of Frank Asch.

BIBLIOGRAPHY
Unit 3
Inspired by an article from *OWL* Magazine, 2001.
Unit 4
National Aeronautics and Space Administration. *Starchild, A Learning Centre for Young Astronomers* on site http://starchild.gsfc.nasa.gov/docs/StarChild.
Canadian Space Agency. "How can I become an astronaut?" on Canadian Astronaut Office - FAQs site http://www.space.gc.ca/asc/eng/astronauts/faq.asp#1.
Unit 7
Public Health Agency of Canada. *Canada's Physical Activity Guide for Youth.* Minister of Public Works and Government Services Canada, 2002.
Unit 8
Environment Canada. "Water Use in the Home" from Environment Canada's Freshwater site www.ec.gc.ca/water. Minister of Public Works and Government Services Canada, 2006.
Unit 11
Canada Career Consortium. *Destination 2020* site http://www.careerccc.org/destination2020/D2020-E.pdf.
Anthology
Asch, Frank. "Summer." From http://www.canteach.ca/elementary/songs poems6.html. Reprinted with permission.
Beyde, Angel. "Lynn Johnston: See You in the Funny Papers!" Original text written for Les Éditions CEC inc., 2006.
Born, Alan for Library and Archives Canada. "Terry Fox." Minister of Public Works and Government Services Canada, 2005.
Brock, Patricia and B.J. Busby for Canada Post. "Laura Secord." Minister of Public Works and Government Services Canada, 1992.
Dunn, William and Guy Trépanier. "Children of the World." In *And The Message Is…* Prentice Hall Ginn Canada, 1997.
Jacobs, W.W. "The Monkey's Paw." In public domain.
Johnston, Lynn. "For Better or for Worse." Lynn Johnston Productions and Universal Press Syndicate, 2005.
Keens-Douglas, Richard. "What Works Best for Me." In *And The Message Is…* Prentice Hall Ginn Canada, 1997.
Kenward, Jean. "E.T." In *Spaceways: An Anthology of Space Poetry*, Oxford University Press, 1985.
Martineau, Josée-Chantal. "A Real Christmas" and "Tiny Men Coming for You." Original texts written for Les Éditions CEC inc., 2006.
Morton, Alexandra. "From a Whale Watcher's Diary." In *Fur, Feathers, Scales and Skin*, Prentice Hall, 1997.
Scrimger, Richard. "Daedalus." Excerpt from "Wings to the Sun," from *Heroes, Deeds and Wonders*, Prentice Hall Ginn Canada, 1998.
Tynes, Maxine. "Save the World for Me." In *Together is Better*, Prentice Hall, 1997.